# BAGHERIA

*By the same author*

Isolina
The Silent Duchess

*Dacia Maraini*

# BAGHERIA

*Translated from the Italian by
Dick Kitto and Elspeth Spottiswood*

PETER OWEN
*London & Chester Springs*

PETER OWEN PUBLISHERS
73 Kenway Road London SW5 0RE
Peter Owen books are distributed in the USA by
Dufour Editions Inc. Chester Springs PA 19425–0007

This edition first published in Great Britain 1994
© 1993 RCS Rizzoli Libri S.p.A., Milano
Translation © Dick Kitto and Elspeth Spottiswood 1994

A catalogue record for this book is available from the British Library

ISBN 0–7206–0926–7

Typeset by The Electronic Book Factory Ltd Fife
Printed in Great Britain by Biddles of Guildford

# BAGHERIA

IT was in 1947 that I saw Bagheria for the first time. I arrived from Palermo where I had come in the boat from Naples, and before that in another boat, an ocean liner, from Tokyo.

Two years of war, two years in a concentration camp: crossing oceans strewn with mines; every day, on deck, drills on how to fling ourselves into the sea in a proper fashion, life-belts round our waists, in case the ship struck a mine.

I still have a snapshot of that boat showing part of the windswept deck and a small girl in a flowered dress flapping round her knees. That child was me. I had short hair so fair it was almost white, and red canvas gym shoes. My hand was being held by an American officer.

I was very popular with the American Marines. I reminded them of the small daughters they had left behind at home. They loaded me with presents, bars of chocolate, big boxes of pea flour, sticks of candy striped red and white.

One of them liked me so much that he took me to his cabin and I went up three flights of stairs behind his thin gawky legs. He showed me photographs of his six-year-old daughter, and then he started to fondle my knees and I took immediate flight. Half-tumbling I fled down all the stairs I had just gone up with him. It was then I learned something about a father's love, at the same time so tender and so lascivious, so overbearing and so gentle.

At night I dreamed of being pursued by an aeroplane that was machine-gunning the passers-by, chasing them as if it were a hawk. It dived down and attacked from behind, leaving in its wake a thrilling flavour of fear and flight and a small cloud of dust raised by the whirring of its wings.

Death and I belonged to each other. I knew her well. I was familiar with her as if she were some idiot cousin whom I would have liked to play with and from whom I could expect anything from a gesture of affection to a kick, a kiss to the thrust of a knife.

My mother's family was waiting for us in Palermo. A dying grandfather, a grandmother with big black eyes, whose life was devoted to the cult of her past beauty, an eighteenth-century villa now in ruins and relations who belonged to the nobility, suspicious and shut away.

On the quayside we got into a carriage that would take us to Bagheria. We loaded it with all our belongings, which were in fact quite meagre, because we had come from Japan, without either money or possessions, stripped bare, with nothing on our backs except the clothes handed out by the American military.

The carriage took us along the via Francesco Crispi, the

via dei Barillai, the via Cala di Porto Carbone, surrounded by broken stubs of houses which had been destroyed in the war. Then Porta Felice with its two beautiful towers, the Foro Italico, once called Marina, next door to the real Piazza Marina, where all the biggest festivals of Palermo had been held and hangings and slaughterings carried out.

Continuing on our way, we turned down the road that runs alongside the sea, full of bends and still not tarred, but in the built-up areas paved with the traditional cobbled stones and elsewhere white with dust and earth. Then we turned away from Monte Pellegrino, rising like a tower above a Palermo that was totally derelict and in ruins. We came to a summer countryside of burned grass and dry, parched watercourses.

Remembering this journey brings a lump to my throat. Why have I never written about it before? Beautiful Bagheria! Almost as if putting the word down on paper would give it a form, as if I could feel it falling on top of me, overwhelming me with a murmur of vanished distances. Is it a mirage? A city seen mirrored and sparkling at the end of a stony road which would vanish into nothingness if one came too close?

I sat between my father, then at the height of his good looks and powers of seduction (later I learned how I could be seduced and tormented by being a daughter in love with her father), and my mother. She too was young and beautiful, still almost a girl with her long fair hair and large bright eyes. In front of me sat my two sisters, one, with her small well-formed head, her almond-shaped eyes almost Chinese with their delicately swelling eyelids, who would be a musician; the other, with little podgy arms and reddish skin studded with freckles, would be a writer.

The horse, all skin and bones, a post-war horse which had to eat spoiled hay because it was cheap, was finding it hard to carry us all, even though there was very little luggage. Yet it seemed to me as if we were rushing at breakneck speed towards the future on those black and red wheels. What did fate hold in store for us?

Having survived the horrors of bombing and desperate hunger, I had also lost my all too frequent association with the idiot cousin – death. I sat calmly on the small padded seat of the carriage and looked round me thinking that anything and everything was possible. I felt curious as I smelled the unaccustomed scent of jasmine mixed with the odour of horse dung.

To the left was the sea, coloured a raw vegetable green. On the right, a flat plain of olives and lemon trees. For the first time I breathed in the air of the island I had heard spoken of so much during our imprisonment in Japan. But more than anything else they had talked of food from morning till night, to satisfy in imagination the hunger that dried up the saliva in our mouths and gave us cramps in our guts.

'Do you remember the pasta with aubergines we used to eat in Palermo? The black glistening slices submerged in sweet tomatoes . . . ?' 'And those other aubergines they called "quails" because they sold them ready-cooked, shaped as if they had wings on each side of their bodies: how they had the flavour of aniseed, and the smell of oil when they were being fried?'

'Do you remember the sardines baked with a stuffing of raisins and pinenuts, and the tender flesh of the fish that flaked off on the tongue?'

'What about those *trionfi di gola*, the little sweet cakes we bought from the nuns along with the pistachio jelly that seemed to penetrate right into the brain, it was so scented and delicate?'

'And do you remember those little cakes shaped like breasts and filled with sweetened ricotta?'

All of a sudden the carriage was threading its way between low houses crowded together, white and blue cubes without windows, with balconies left unfinished on the roof in case another floor might be added. Was this Ficarazzi?

Every so often in the middle of that huddle of minute houses, a sudden vision: a large villa of rose-coloured tufa stone with scrolls incised on the walls and statues on the roof, long flights of steps opening out like a fan, fake windows, fake balustrades – everything a game of pretence for the restless eyes of the gentlemen of past centuries, a balance between fullness and emptiness, which seems to suggest a teasing out of subtle architectural mysteries.

There was the elegance of the *trompe-l'oeil* design, and the wretched poverty of hovels built for sheer existence: walls of stone knocked up by hand without so much as the hint of a trained architect to keep an eye on them. It seemed as if the walls only stayed upright because they were all leaning against each other.

At times the road led through vines and one could see nothing but bunches of grapes and vine leaves. Then suddenly, a bend in the road and we were close to the sea, almost skimming alongside it. You could see the white pebbles and the water lazily covering and uncovering them with a gentle, desultory movement.

In Japan I never went to the sea. At first we had been at Sapporo amongst the snows of eternal winter. There were days in January when we had to climb out of the house through the window because the door was buried under a heap of frozen snow. Later we were transferred to Kyoto where I learned to speak the local dialect. Then to Nagoya and the bombs.

How can I ever forget the grim splendour of those explosions? The night lit up by balls of blinding light falling slowly, slowly, as if they did not know whether they were going up or coming down. But the aeroplanes did know exactly how to make use of that hovering light which enabled them to target their bombs at a time when everyone was asleep.

The hiss of bombs ripping through the night air. And then, a distant boom. I learned to distinguish the dangerous bombs from the less threatening ones. And with the fierce intensity of someone who thinks only of their survival hanging day by day on a thread, I enjoyed the marvellous sight of those nocturnal jousts above the neighbouring town. I knew how on other nights it would be our turn to be highlighted and we would fling ourselves out of bed and streak to the shelter while shards of deadly shrapnel flew around like flies in the night air.

After a year of bombing, with the sensation of walking suspended on a tight-rope, expecting to lose our lives as easily as one might lose a tooth, with feet taut and motionless above the void, the Japanese soldiers came and took us to another concentration camp. But this time it was in the country, inside a Buddhist temple. There I became familiar with the rice-paddies infested with snakes and leeches. I knew the sultry atmosphere of afternoons when we were half-starved, and the dream of a fresh juicy peach became so compelling that it would make you bite your own hand.

Then the question arose whether or not it had been wise to refuse to subscribe to the Fascist Republic of Salo without thinking 'how it might affect the children who have nothing to do with politics'. My mother said that in the eyes of some of the starving men, our fellow companions in the camp, there was a flicker of cannibal desire as they stared at the tender flesh of her youngest daughter, barely a year old.

My father replied that this was one of the consequences of our anti-fascism and we could only wait till the end of the war, which the Allies would win, without any doubt.

'And if they lose?' In that case we knew we would be faced with a brutal death, probably at gunpoint.

'Don't talk about it in front of the children.'

'Everything will be all right, you'll see.'

'And if it's not?'

In the dark I could hear them stubbornly bickering in the one room where we all slept together. And in my heart I felt they were just children. But I would rather be there with them than anywhere else without them. I watched and brooded over them, my two young parents who looked up at the sky and could not see where to put their feet.

I had already become used to playing with stones; the big ones were for big helpings and the little ones for little helpings. They were carefully painted and sometimes it was possible to appease my hunger through my eyes. At the same time I also learned to pull out of my bottom the long plump worms which were inside me eating the small amount of rice that was our only food in the camp.

I knew nothing of the sea, although Japan consists of islands, and fish and seaweed form an essential part of the national diet. We had always lived in the interior: woods of maple trees with their star-shaped leaves (was it Karisawa with its ice-cold sweet-smelling waters?), temples with pillars of red-lacquered wood, rivers of black sand with swarms of lemon-yellow butterflies flying above them.

It was only then that I got to know the sea, that maternal and elusive body, malign and yet benevolent, and I fell in love with it for always. I soon learned to play on the rocks, leaping away from the big waves with a jump and plunging through the turbulent breakers a moment before they hurled themselves ferociously against the rocks, hunting for sea-urchins under water, catching crabs and shrimps in pools edged with a salt crust, my feet in the warm seaweed that sent out a scorched smell I shall never forget.

'Here is Cattolica,' said my mother, 'we've almost arrived.' A large villa with elegant flights of steps, windows without frames like empty eye-sockets, walls cracked and crumbling, clouds of powdery dust. A garden left to grow old, the blades of fruiting cactus plants smothered in dust, interspersed with delicate bushes of jasmine, sudden explosions of fiery-red hibiscus flowers, a bougainvillaea of phosphorescent purple that no one had tended for years and was stubbornly determined to climb up over the ruined walls. Further on, the big cement works and the pasta factory, white dust belching from its gratings, dribbling from the high windows and from the gutters, floating down along the outside walls of the building, growing darker as it reached street level.

In those days one came into Bagheria from below, passing over the level crossing whose gates remained shut for minutes on end beneath the blazing sun, amidst a whirlwind of flies and mosquitoes.

The carriage stopped in front of the closed gates at the level crossing. My father got down to stretch his legs. Meanwhile the driver talked to his horse, encouraging it to complete its stint in spite of the heat, the flies, the exhaustion and the minute amount of food given to it for survival.

To the right stood a gigantic fig tree from which hung little wrinkled bags whitened by dust; it seemed to bar the way for bicycles coming from Aspra. To the left, a glimpse of the station with its gleaming rails; in front, devastated by enormous holes, the road leading up to the Villa Butera.

The horse, its ribs protruding on either side of its back, shook its head in distress to chase away the flies; as if it were saying 'no' to the hill in front of it, 'no' to the tarred road that was softened by the sun and sank beneath its hooves, and 'no' to the sultry heat, the dust, hunger and drudgery.

We climbed up the hill on foot. The horse, after more than fifteen kilometres, could not go any further and the driver was afraid it would collapse. So we set off along the Corsa Butera looking at the people of Bagheria just as they were looking at us, even though we were more accepting and they were more suspicious and puzzled about us. At one point we heard a little boy shouting 'Look, a woman in trousers!' My mother was indeed wearing loose trousers for travelling, and this was looked on as scandalous.

There were hardly any cars to be seen. Instead the traffic consisted of carts drawn by mules and donkeys ridden by men with severe frowning expressions, wearing dark-coloured clothes, their faces also darkened by the sun. There were women almost all dressed in black: seven years of mourning for the death of a father, three years for the death of a brother, and for the death of a husband, mourning for the rest of a woman's life. They walked with quick inviting footsteps among the dozens of children who flitted like flies through the village.

In the Piazza Madrice we stopped for a moment to get back our breath. My mother had told me that inside the church there was a cradle of gilded wood, shaped like a big shell, supported on the wings of a flying eagle and surrounded by flying cupids. It had been a present from the Princess Butera to the village of Bagheria. My mother still remembers that cradle, but however hard I looked for it, I never managed to find it.

Meanwhile the driver, walking alongside his horse, had caught up with us and told us that it was all right if we wanted to get back into the carriage. So, sitting on the uncomfortable folding seats, we took the road towards the Villa Palagonia.

Corso Umberto revealed all the poverty and suffering of the bitter post-war years: battered houses, wretched-looking shops, a convent, a school, and a café consisting of a bare ugly room without windows, separated from the street by a curtain made of plaited string. The big attraction was the Emporium, where they sold everything from soap flakes to mint-flavoured caramels, from sherbet to raisins, from wax candles to the little Walt Disney pigs in china that I liked so much and which my mother found 'absolutely hideous and in deplorable taste'.

This was my first encounter with popular taste. 'But what is deplorable taste?' I asked my mother. What makes a thing ugly? And after having been so long associated with books and objects of refined taste, why does one come to regard as ugly what children and most ordinary people see as beautiful? For years I was obsessed with this thought about the ugliness of the many and the beauty of the select few, searching for answers to questions that still do not seem to have any explanation. Can there be an art that does not originate from the distillation of good taste, from the basis of a profound knowledge of its subject, from the vicissitudes of a long apprenticeship to beauty? I was convinced of my mother's viewpoint, but then the sixties came and turned upside-down all the old beliefs, with the dream that art can be both spontaneous and popular.

In the houses of my school friends I used to see lampstands in the form of provocative Venuses, ashtrays that imitated a small cupped hand, little tapestries of pastoral scenes, large hand-coloured photographs of dead people, *ex voto* pictures depicting badly drawn parts of the human body, and much else in dubious taste. But just as I fell for the insipid songs that drooled on about love, I was filled with admiration for the embroidered antimacassars on the backs of armchairs, for shoes that exactly matched handbags, for showy bracelets in the form of serpents, and for a little enamelled plate on which was inscribed 'After three days the guest will stink'. I could not understand why these small delights of popular taste did not appeal to my mother; I divided myself carefully in half, hiding my preferences when I was with her

*17*

and exaggerating them in front of my school friends from Bagheria.

Fortunately our house contained no books of a similar kind to these objects, or I would have read them all avidly and filled my head with nonsense. I was hungry for books and devoured everything that fell into my hands. On the bookshelves of our home I found Lucretius, Tacitus, Shakespeare, Dickens, Conrad, Faulkner, Steinbeck, Dreiser, Melville. They were mostly English and American books, because my father, having an English mother, had always preferred to read books in English. In this way I ranged from Mickey Mouse (at that time sold in throw-away pocket books) to Henry James without feeling out of my element.

As for films, I still remember the first time a projector reappeared in Bagheria after a fire in the Cinema Moderno. It was set up in front of the church, and at least a hundred people crowded round in a fever of astonishment to see this great marvel, a sequence of white ectoplasm moving on the walls of the church.

Then things became more organized. Instead of the church wall, a sort of arena was constructed; seats made of cactus leaves were dotted about at the back, a sheet was stretched up as a screen, and on it easily recognizable American cowboys on horseback would gallop after Red Indians with feathered head-dresses. Some time afterwards a proper cinema was built, with folding wooden seats, and every time someone got up the seats would hit the back with a loud bang.

Little by little, as passionate love, kissing and embracing became more central to the films, women were likely to be excluded. It was considered improper for girls to go to the cinema, even if they were accompanied. In later years I remember going with my father to see a film starring Esther Williams, whom I very much admired. The audience was all boys and youths, apart from a few old men with berets rammed down over their heads. They talked incessantly at the top of their voices, and whenever two actors came close to a kiss, they started to shout 'Get her! Get her!' And there were peals of laughter, raspberries and much hand-clapping. For a young girl it was difficult to endure the bawdy atmosphere without the fear of being considered shameless.

Many years later, during the 1980s when I was in Palermo doing some research on the theatres of the city, I went with the architect Marilù Balsamo to visit the former Finocchiaro Theatre which had become a red-light cinema. When we went to the box-office to ask if we could see inside the theatre, they gaped at us, scandalized.

'But we'll pay the entrance tickets if you want.'

'No. Women aren't allowed in.'

'Why on earth not?'

'The place is for men only. They would be horrified to see a woman, let alone two together. And how could we guarantee your safety if they tried to get at you?'

The depiction of sex was not on for women, either then or now.

On that afternoon of 1947, the driver of the carriage came to a halt in front of the gates to the Villa Valguarnera, swearing at the hill, the heat and the flies. A plump woman opened the gates for us. It was Innocenza, with her warm affectionate laugh, whom I would come to know well. She cried out, 'Signor Boscu, signora Popopazia, signorina Raci, signorina Ciunka, signorina Ntoni! Welcome to Bagheria!'

Later we would learn how the people of Bagheria displayed the vigour of their dialect by completely mispronouncing the names of people and things alike. 'Signor Boscu' was my father Fosco, 'Popopazia' my mother Topazia, 'Raci' was me, 'Ciunka' my sister Yuki, and 'Ntoni' my sister Toni.

IN the villa awaiting us was my Grandmother Sonia, with her broad pallid face and her big black eyes encircled with dark smoky rings like the heroines in Murnau's films; Grandfather Enrico, who had been bedridden for several months; Aunt Orietta, with her sweet smile and a twitch in her right shoulder that gave the impression that she was always trying to shrug off the world; and Uncle Gianni, with his intelligent sad eyes.

Our accommodation was in the former stables, three small rooms beneath the arcades with a bathroom the size of a beach hut and small square windows that looked out over the hen run.

Our greatest joy was a little door opening on to four steps that led up to the garden of the villa. If it had not been for that garden, our house would really have been impossibly restricted. As it was, the moment we got out of bed we would hurl ourselves up the four steps to run along between the scented flowerbeds and enjoy the breath-taking view of the valley of olive trees sloping down towards the sea.

At that time I spoke more Japanese than Italian, and I had to struggle through the verbal hazards of dialect to learn Italian grammar, mixing the Sicilian of nursery rhymes and proverbs with the English of my favourite sea stories. At school I never managed to get started and never paid attention, and anyway I spent my time poring over books. I skimmed through my homework so that I could get back to Captain Nemo and the White Whale.

One day a priest held me close and gave me a hasty kiss on the mouth. After that I was never able to unravel the tangle between faith and morality. At home we were not Catholic, and there was an idea that mankind was a chance product of nature and chaos, an intelligent descendant from monkeys and 'sea-lice', as my father used to say.

But what I learned from the nuns at school sounded fascinating and made more sense than the abstract ideas of my parents. Secretly I even made a small altar with a miniature statue of Our Lady which was totally conventional in appearance: blue veil, eyes raised to Heaven, an impenetrable expression, a baby at her breast and a serpent beneath her feet. I used to kneel down before it and pray for 'all unbelievers'. At the same time, the war had left me with an irrational fear of the night and of silence. Whenever my father and mother were late coming home, I tortured myself imagining their bodies wounded, bleeding, dismembered, mangled, and until I heard their voices I had no peace.

My sisters and I still played with stones and leaves, as we had done in the concentration camp. We did not know what toys were, and when we were given presents of dolls they seemed like a luxury that wasn't meant for us. For years, whenever there was any bread left over, I used to hide it just as dogs do. I would put lumps of sugar in the bottom of drawers and later I would find them crumbling and swarming with ants. I used to bury pieces of marzipan wrapped in paper underneath trees so that I could get them when I felt hungry.

But the hunger of the camp was over. Now we could eat, even if only very simply because we were so poor; meat just once a month, fruit that we bought direct from the peasants, and as much pasta as we wanted, seasoned with olive oil and salt or sometimes oil and anchovies.

We wore shoes that were continually being resoled and clothes that were turned inside out. For years I wore a coat that was made out of an old jacket of my grandfather's. My mother said it was made of good English wool, indestructible. I would have given anything for it to have been a bit more destructible.

Even a dentist, a good one, cost more than we could afford. I remember one horrible occasion when a peasant dentist had to extract a bad tooth and was pulling and chiselling and sweating more or less as I imagined he would have done a century earlier. Anaesthetics were for the 'grand doctors', and I had to have my teeth pulled out like the other children in Bagheria, with ordinary pincers and afterwards a sweet popped straight into my mouth to stop me crying.

It was not long before my grandfather died and my mother and my aunt wept inconsolably. He had been a man of great generosity and kindness of heart; a man of wide reading and refined tastes, an amateur philosopher and a connoisseur of wine.

We stayed on at the Villa Valguarnera for some time, quarrelling with my grandmother, who did not like us and could not bear having to put up with us. Finally we moved to a slightly larger house in Porticello only ten metres from the sea. There I remember the continuous sound of the waves beating on the rocks, at times discordant and even threatening; cold winters alleviated by a stove which was always smoking, and timeless mornings among the rocks fishing for those small transparent shrimps that hide in pools of salt water.

My father had started to work again and with his first salary he bought himself a small sailing boat in which we used to go off together out to sea. I stayed at the tiller and he dived into the sea to look for grouper fish among the rocks. He would emerge like a Triton, lustrous and dripping, with big fishes dangling from his belt.

Later everything collapsed; I don't know how, I don't know why. He disappeared, leaving behind him the heart of a child in love, beset by sad and heavy thoughts. My mother had to bring up the children on her own, surrounded by piles of accumulated debts and overdrafts that were forever falling due, taking away our sleep and our appetites.

THE name Bagheria is thought to come from the Arabic *bab el gherib* meaning 'the gate of the wind'. Others, however, say that Bagheria derives from the word *baharia* which means 'the seashore'.

I prefer to think of it as 'the gate of the wind' because Bagheria has not much in the way of seashore even though the sea is only a kilometre away from the town. It was created, with its splendid architecture, as a country retreat for the nobility of Palermo during the eighteenth century. It has kept something of the atmosphere of a summer garden enriched by lemon groves and olive trees, poised between the hills, cooled by the salt winds coming from the direction of Capo Zafferano.

I try to imagine Bagheria as it was before the random development of the fifties, before the systematic destruction of its beauty; and earlier still, before the famine and the plagues when it were the favourite summer resort for the nobility of Palermo. In the distant past it had resembled the mother of antiquity, from whose womb the town and all around it were born. Writing one hundred years before Christ, the Greek historian Polybius spoke of great wooded expanses 'near Panormo' as the scene of a battle between the Carthaginians and republican Rome.

Between Mount Cannita, where the city of Kponia apparently arose as a place devoted to the cult of the goddess Athene, and the Cozzo Porcara, where the remains of a Phoenician necropolis have been found, there was this 'small and pleasant valley', later called Bagheria. It is triangular in shape, with the rocky point of Capo Zafferano rising out of the sea like the prow of a ship. One side takes in the villages of Santa Flavia, Porticello and Sant'Elia: until after the war, the other side, wilder and lashed by the sea, encompassed only the village of Aspra, with fishing boats drawn up out of the water on the white sand. In the centre, lying between the hills, surrounded by a mass of olive and lemon trees, is Bagheria, lapped by the river Eleuterio, which today is reduced to a trickle. In the time of Polybius this river was navigable right down to the sea.

Holm oaks, cork oaks, ash, nut trees, figs and carobs, almonds, and fruiting cactuses were the most widespread plants and trees. And the eye could stretch from one side of the triangle to the other, between light and dark shades of green, imagining that a naked giant with one eye in the middle of his forehead might suddenly spring out of nowhere.

Today the view is horribly disfigured: trees, parks, gardens and ancient buildings have been hacked down to make way for houses and large tasteless mansions. Something still remains of the old greatness of Bagheria, but only in isolated fragments between the vestiges of abandoned villas, amidst the obscenity of new motorways that have forced a way right into the centre of the town, savagely destroying gardens, fountains, and everything that exists beneath one's feet.

My mother has told me that when she was a little girl there used to be a Carthusian monastery inside the Villa Butera. 'It was a monastery in miniature, with all the rooms and chapels of a real monastery. When you went in, you would be met by a lay brother carrying a jar of water. Then you'd go further down the corridor and you'd be able to look into the cells where monks with cassocks down to their feet were intent on praying or writing. They seemed absolutely real but they were made of wax filled with straw. In the middle of the prayer hall there was even a bear with a head that could move.

'The walls were decorated with paintings in the style of Velázquez. There was also an old manservant wearing slippers and draped in aprons, who was busily sweeping the paving stones in the courtyard. In one of the larger cells a supper party was displayed: Admiral Horatio Nelson and Queen Maria Carolina were being served by a black footman. There was a kitchen too, with a cook busily frying two eggs in a pan. In another room the Norman King Roger was perusing a manuscript. And at the end, in the dining-hall, was the Prince Branciforte, sitting at table and calmly talking with Louis XVI and the Bourbon Ferdinand the First. People used to come from everywhere to visit the Monastery of Bagheria. But do they come now?'

Today the monastery is no more. I have no idea who was responsible for its destruction. But Bagheria has such a poor opinion of itself that it does not attach any importance to its most valued memories.

It has always been thought that the Sicilians possess a certain darkness of character, a dry, sullen mentality springing from the earth which generates them. The frequent violence of their political behaviour can only stem from those inaccessible grey and rugged rocks, that hostile overpowering sea, that rough dry countryside, arid and deathly, from the great treeless fields of grain without any shelter from the sun. Out of ruined walls bristling with thorns emerges the agave plant, raising its beautiful head to the sky in a transparent spike of scented flowers only at the heart-rending moment of its death.

If you read the writers of antiquity you discover that it has not always been like this. Once there were luxuriant streams, woods of great leafy trees, hard-working people passing to and fro beneath their restful shade. They spoke a language that would be incomprehensible today, they ate bread cooked on stones and drank wine diluted with water and mixed with honey, and they laughed at heaven knows what, showing their white teeth and their dark eyes.

Under those leafy branches walked Phoenicians, and they tell me it was perhaps they who gave Bagheria its name from the Phoenician word *bayaria* meaning 'return': or so I am told. But it is difficult to be sure of the truth; etymology is frequently a mystery.

Under these branches Greeks and Romans also used to walk; and eventually fleet-footed Arabs with their long robes of embroidered cotton. The Arabs brought to Sicily the silk-worm, the olive and the fruiting cactus. The Spaniards brought the cultivation of sweet oranges along with their horses and their warriors, and at the same time the Aragonese introduced the use of sugar cane.

As a child I used to go into the fields around the villa with a group of children from Bagheria to look for mulberries; our dresses would become stained with the juice and we would get a scolding from our mothers. But these soft, swelling berries that coloured your tongue blue and red were irresistible.

Today there are no more mulberries in Bagheria. They have all been cut down. But on the quay at Mondello along the coast from Palermo, it is still possible to find fruit stalls where for a few coins they will sell you a bag made of sugar paper with a handful of juicy mulberries inside.

The mulberry was also the tree that consoled me during the two years in the concentration camp at Nagoya. Every day the guards used to put us all into a queue and count us. But sometimes they used to forget us children, and I would take advantage of their oversight to squeeze through the barbed wire and run off to the peasants to work for a few hours, happy to be rewarded with an onion and a piece of *daikon*, a sort of radish that lay motionless on the plate, white and twisted like a small corpse, with a taste of putrid water which I hated. But it was better then being hungry.

*Daikon* also resembled ginseng which in its turn brings to mind a dwarf with thin legs and thread-like arms: like a little man or a new-born baby with very white soft limbs. But no one ever points out that mandrake was just the same. So much confused information lies embedded in the memory, and often we don't attempt to question it. Today I know that mandrake is a poisonous herb with white flowers, segmented leaves and large tuberous roots to which magical properties were once attributed.

In the fourteenth century, I believe it was called *mandragora*. Then, no one knows how, it was changed to *mandragola*. In Latin it was pronounced *mandragoram* and in Greek *mandragoras*. But there is also a suggestion that the word comes from the Persian *mardum-gia*, meaning 'plant of man'.

In the concentration camp I learned to understand the deep-rooted ironic relationship that exists between food and the magic of the imagination. It is starvation that makes the senses reel and fantasy dance. It is deprivation that is the origin of all desire and also of all the more or less secret distortions of our thinking.

Having to eat *daikon* was enough to make me cry. But I also knew it was the only fresh vegetable that ever arrived on our table and we had to make the best of it. I still remember how I used to sit miserable and paralysed and full of hatred in front of a small dish of boiled *daikon*, while tears welled up involuntarily and, sliding down my hollow cheeks, ended up in my lap. I saw *daikon* as evil, white and repugnant, even though it did me good. Its roots stirred my poor empty stomach with agonizing cramps. So I used to put off the moment when I forced them into my mouth. *Daikon* would stay there mutely on the plate and pretend to be dead. But far from it. It was still very much alive. Doesn't *daikon* make one think of *daimon*? A small demon with flesh that appears white and innocent, a faked innocence which was camouflaged in the plain earthenware dishes of the camp.

I was happiest when I was able to play among the peasants. I used to slip my small hands into the huge basket where the men had thrown mulberry leaves. I would pull them out, light and slightly downy, and spread them over the beds of little grubs. These small creatures were silkworms; they were blind and touchy and stayed shut inside their cocoons made of something very like a spider's web, which stuck to the fingers and gave out a faint smell of flour and cut grass.

Sometimes I would hold one in the palm of my hand before it had become imprisoned in its nest of opaque spittle. I remember the extraordinary softness of its tiny body, almost as if its flesh were made out of clouds. My hands are good at retaining the memory of anything they touch. They are small dry hands with the nails always cut very short, my little finger much smaller than the others. The veins stand out as if I used my hands a lot: indeed my fingers flit backwards and forwards on the keyboard of my electronic typewriter for hours on end. I have worked hard trying to learn how to balance the weight of my fingers on the keys. In order to use the little finger I had to bend my hands askew and push my wrists out. In the end I decided to give up and now I have abandoned using the little fingers and type only with the other eight.

The tepid floury softness of the silkworm, almost ready to disintegrate in my fingers – I found it again when for the first time in my life I held a penis in my hand. A family friend

*29*

who, like the American Marine had done, took advantage of a moment when we were alone to unzip his trousers and put his penis in my hand. I looked at it with curiosity, not at all frightened. We were in Bagheria and I was ten years old. Since it was clear that he did not want to touch my body (which I would have found abhorrent), but only gently and trustingly to show me his, I was not upset. It was the first penis I had ever seen. How strange it is that the word *pene* (penis) should be so close to the word *pena* (pain). Who knows whether using the word penis is not also a way of insinuating that the bearer of a penis is also a bearer of pain? But maybe this is only a fluke of language.

Seeing a penis for the first time brought me some slight pain. I was only a child and he was imposing his grown-up body on me, even though there was no violence, and this man was a good friend of the family, a frequent visitor to the house.

Up till then I had only once caught a glimpse of my father's penis, but it was in repose and was not being offered to me. Indeed, he was shamed by my glance and immediately covered himself in embarrassment. And my dear father was never shameless. Throughout my childhood I gave him my love without its being returned. My love was a solitary love. I watched over him, his secret smells, over his every footprint, never to be retraced.

He was forever on his travels, forever far away. I transformed my longing into an intricate, airy architecture, into the mirage of a city and the desire to dream with open eyes. Whenever he came back from one of his journeys I took meticulous note of the smells he brought back with him, the smell of apples (why does the inside of haversacks always have that strong musty underlying smell of apples?), of dirty washing, of hair warmed by the sun, of crumpled books, dry bread, old shoes, withered flowers, tobacco, and tiger balsam against rheumatism.

The combined smell was not unpleasant, indeed it had a

unique sweetness about it. It is a smell that today still makes my heart leap whenever I come across it in some corner of the house, in some old garment, in some shoulder bag cast to one side. It was the smell of a solitary man, impatient of all ties, of all responsibilities, who travelled ceaselessly from one continent to another; a pilgrim with Spartan tastes, used to sleeping on the ground, to living on almost nothing, abstemious and sober but capable of much eating and drinking if he were in good company on the top of a mountain or in an abandoned bathing-hut among the rocks beside the sea. Occasionally he would smoke a pipe, but I was not conscious of the smell of tobacco in his clothes – only once in a while in his 'rucksack', as it came to be called in the family. In the concentration camp he and the other men used to smoke rolled-up cherry leaves which tasted hot and bitter. But I liked the smell; it had a light flowery scent.

I loved my father so much, more than it is right to love a father, with a painful torment – as if I anticipated in my heart the distance that would later separate us, his old age that already seemed intolerable, an image of his death which would leave me inconsolable, but of which I saw the shadow between his delicate eyelashes, between his untamed thoughts, in the corners of his subtle delicate lips.

'What's this white stuff that's coming out of your body?' I asked the family friend who was bent over with a jerk of pleasure while his silkworm swelled between my hands and, after a quiver, began to grow smaller, leaving a white sticky fluid in my child's palm.

He smiled. He did not know what to say to me. Or perhaps he said something like 'you'll understand later, when you're grown-up'. For a moment I thought it was an illness, a purulent eruption, something secret and unnatural which threatened his health. I was so astounded by the sudden metamorphosis of the little worm that I thought 'he must have swallowed a piece of mushroom like Alice. Now he'll eat another piece and it will become big and strong again. There was definitely something startling and unexpected in this growing and diminishing of flesh in a grown-up person. And I still did not know it was called a penis.

Then for days on end this friend of the family was not to be seen. And I thought with a mixture of repulsion and curiosity about the way his body had leaned forward, of that spurt of milk that had dirtied my hands, of the shameful expression on his face as it bent strangely above me but without touching me, as if his detached closeness demonstrated that he was separate from what he was doing.

His act of putting such a soft and defenceless worm into my hand I saw then as one of total trust, and it made me feel proud of myself. When I met him again, some time later, he seemed severe and he drew away from me. He told me off for being a precocious little girl, too nosey, given to forward behaviour. And he succeeded in convincing my mother, to such an extent that he induced her to throw away a sleeveless dress with a short skirt which I was very attached to, in order to make a longer one with pleats, which I hated.

Years later, during the seventies and eighties, I found myself with friends in one of the 'self-awareness' groups (as they were then called) that formed the backbone of the women's movement. We would meet for lunch or supper when we were free of our respective jobs, and we talked for hours on end, taking turns to analyse methodically our earliest experiences connected with the discovery of sex, love, the desire for children and so on. It was then I discovered that so-called sexual abuse of children by adults was very common and well known to all, or almost all, little girls. They often kept quiet about it for the rest of their lives, terrified by threats and intimidations from the men who had taken them into dark corners, always feeling guilty as if it was they who had stretched out their hands, conceived forbidden thoughts and provoked the uncertain desires of men, even though the reality was quite the opposite. And once it came to light, they had to struggle with incredulous mothers who were ready to lay all the blame on their daughters, instead of on fathers, lovers, cousins, brothers, and friends of the family.

Such is the trauma that most women just blot it out of their memory and it can take years of therapy to bring it into the open. After ten years of psychotherapy, a friend of mine found out how as a child she had been abused by her grandfather. But she had conveniently 'forgotten' it to keep the peace in the family and to avoid upsetting her mother.

It has been a relief and a source of mutual knowledge to learn that it is not a solitary, isolated experience, but underlying it there is a universal system with established techniques for keeping little girls silent and shut away inside their 'dirty' secrets, as if they were responsible for the precarious family happiness. We have initiated a shared discourse on the age-old violence of patriarchy and the men who have always considered it their right and destiny to possess and manipulate the women of their household.

T HE *senia* or *novia*, now in disuse, consisted of an
arrangement of small buckets attached to a length of
chain which rotated round a mechanical drum. This was
pulled by an animal (usually a donkey or a mule) and
controlled by means of a hand-operated lever. This system
was once used to draw up pails of water for the irrigation
of the fields.

I read this in a book on Bagheria by Oreste Girgenti, the
only really comprehensive book to have recounted the history
of this small town. This Girgenti was obviously an upright
man and much attached to his birthplace, even if it is evident

that in spite of the accuracy of his research, he had a terror of offending the local élite whether they were mayors, the clergy or university professors. It is an authentic and convincing account but absolutely obsequious to authority.

Although the date of the book is given as 1985, I imagine that it is a reprint because it bears all the marks of having come from the drawers of a nineteenth-century writing desk. The photographs with their sober black and white seem to belong to that time, and they portray a Bagheria no longer in existence, with a long queue of students from the Manzoni College, and a glimpse of villas seen from afar, submerged among olive trees that have been cut down for at least half a century. Nothing is said by the worthy Girgenti about the ruination of the town of Bagheria which he still loves and admires.

'Everything started with the development authorized by the town council towards the middle of the nineteen fifties,' writes Francesco Alliata who, together with his young niece Vittoria, is one of the few among my relations to have demonstrated a social conscience. 'My aunt Caterina and my brother Giuseppe were unsuccessful in persuading the council to develop another zone nearby.' The pretext was the construction of an elementary school. But clearly this was just an excuse because the school could perfectly well have been built further away, while the restricted land that surrounded the Villa Valguarnera was an obstacle to anyone who wanted to build right in the centre of Bagheria.

One of the most precious green zones, a delightful area created by the gardeners of three hundred years ago, was thus brutally cleared of its ancient trees, its fountains, its little paths, its statues and sandstone balustrades, to make space for a hideous school when there was no necessity for it to be there at all. But this was merely the first strategic move, ostensibly arising from a consideration of community welfare – for who would be opposed to the building of a state school?

– and would be followed later by an estate of villas and large mansions.

The development of the land was restricted by precise laws aimed at the preservation of the landscape, the monuments and the public gardens, but these were completely disregarded. This first expropriation was followed by the construction of a street, and then by a wider street, and eventually by uncontrolled building.

Only in 1965, when the damage had already been done, did a commission of enquiry arrive from Palermo. After looking into the matter for several months they compiled a crushing series of reports. They listed everyone concerned, with their full surnames and Christian names, and denounced all those who had been involved in the devastation of the first of those two 'green lungs' of Bagheria, and who had attempted to curry favour with the racketeers who in Rome are called *palazzinari*, behaving with an underhand duplicity that was sometimes quite shameless and at other times furtively hidden from the local government officials.

'The communal administration', writes Rosario La Duca, one of the most perceptive observers of conditions in Sicily,

has wilfully ignored the legal procedures that were in force at the time in order to pave the way for private speculation. It has provided a startling example of political malpractice and corruption. . . . Following that of the Villa Butera, the massacre of Bagheria proceeded without interruption. . . . As a result of this enquiry the town council was summoned in front of the magistrates to reply to the grave charges emerging from the proceedings of the scrupulous and vigilant commission of enquiry.

Somebody even accused Francesco Alliata of being involved and of having participated, through his aunt and his cousin Marianna Alliata, in selling off the zones, the 'green lungs' of Bagheria. 'Even if my relations were guilty,' he had replied prudently, 'it was in any event the duty of a serious and responsible town council to stop them, in so much as it should have been acting as custodian and administrator of the laws controlling land development that have been imposed by the State.'

Thanks to my friendship with Professor Antonio Morreale, an impassioned student of Sicilian history and one of the most straightforward, likeable and intelligent people in Bagheria, I have in my hands the 1965 report of the commission of enquiry into the activities of the office of public works in the commune of Bagheria. Reading these papers one is astonished by the glaring arrogance of these communal administrators, who behaved without scruples and without shame, with confidence in their immunity.

'The greatest manipulation regarding the parcelling-out of land in Bagheria', say the commissioners, 'took place in July 1963.' The person who emerges only a few pages later and who continues to appear behind every project, every ambiguous contract and every allocation of land, is the engineer Nicolò Giammanco. An obscure character, threatening and tenacious, who compelled everyone, whether they were honest or dishonest, to do exactly what he wanted. He had something of a devil about him, very like that secret and unhappy character in Sologub's Russian novel *The Little Demon*.

The commissioners interrogated members of the town council, including the mayor, but no one knew a thing, no one remembered a single thing. Some even refused to present themselves. They gave out that they were obliged to be away, they barricaded themselves at home on the pretext that they were ill. One of the town clerks candidly declared that he did not recollect ever having participated in a meeting of the council when there had been any discussion of the price agreed for the area of land on which the school would be built, let alone of any extension of the building zone beyond that designated on the development plan. He added it was probable that these matters had been discussed after the proceedings officially listed on the agenda had come to an end and for this reason he had already left.

But where had he gone? Into the corridor to 'smoke a cigarette' – or did he shut himself in the lavatory waiting for them to finish tampering with the plan approved by the council, or did he go back home? This was not mentioned in the papers of the commission.

'The fact is that this sort of affair', declared the town clerk, 'was always happening, and I remember that every time the council discussed any matter to do with public works, it called on the assistance of an official from the technical office, and this official was almost always the engineer Giammanco.'

The mayor, interrogated in his turn, said he knew nothing of the matter. Everything had fallen from the clouds, almost as if the council was only made up of empty bodies whose brains and memories had been left outside the door.

These are some of the facts, among those related by the commission, that came close to being farcical and would have made one laugh if they had not made one weep on account of the results that ensued, bringing poverty to the citizens of Bagheria, the ruination of the beauty and thus the wealth of the town through the destruction of its architecture and its surroundings.

The town council, for the sake of saying something, eventually awarded the contract to build a secondary school in the middle of the restricted zone to the firm of Barone. This firm began to fell the ancient trees, to excavate foundations and fill them with concrete. But after several months the town council 'recognized' that the work should not go forward because the zone was a restricted one and according to the law no buildings, either public or private, were allowed to be constructed in it.

The said Barone rightly demanded compensation. The

magistrates found for the firm, and the town council was required to pay, since, 'being fully conversant with the afore-mentioned restrictions, they had contracted with the firm of Barone in terms that anticipated the possibility of inter-vention by the competent authority to suspend the work already begun, and to make any necessary adjustments to the plan'.

But everyone knew this was only a temporary hitch, not really to be taken seriously, and that a way would be found to dodge the requirements of the law. A few threats, a few hand-outs of 'black' money and the work would be started once again. Right in the restricted zone, without any permission from the building authority, they began to dig the foundations for a monster ten-storey building, and the plans were regularly approved by the assessors, the buil-ding commission, and the technical officers from the town council.

But the engineer Giammanco had a finger in every pie. The commission of enquiry had straight away discovered that 'an investigation carried out in the restricted zone resulted in a part of the road being enclosed within the property of the engineer Nicolò Giammanco'.

This Giammanco had become friendly with Princess Alliata, and together they had planned an extension of the housing plots 'at the top of the Via Seconda in spite of the existing embargo that the same Alliata had brought to the knowledge of the council in a letter dated 24.8.57'.

The commission discovered that the licences of the planning department, under the direction of the engineer Trovato, were in the handwriting of the engineer Giammanco and also signed in his name. Furthermore, 'all the regulations were left incom-plete, the issue of building permits was irregular, the approval of the Authority was missing, the deposit on the accounts for reinforced concrete was missing from the Prefecture as were any records of regular meetings of the building commissioners, and the payment of any dues to the insurance company for the engineers and architects'.

All the subsequent contracts with members of the public were written in the presence of the notary Di Liberto Di Chiara from Bagheria, 'assisted by the engineer Nicolò Giammanco who is described as a "technical consultant"'. This resulted in their total control of the speculative development in the zoned areas. 'Furthermore, some of the building plots were acquired by the above-mentioned Giammanco.'

The planning department, alerted by the report of the commission (but would it not have been feasible for them to have been aware of it earlier?) declared that permission to build in the restricted zone would never be granted. But evidently no one took the least notice of this declaration since it was during that period that the local administration authorized the new building plots along the Via Seconda and allowed the construction of large new houses in the green belt.

In short, the terms of the commission, like those of the planning department, remained a dead letter. The work continued its outrageous expansion and the two 'green lungs' of Bagheria were 'swallowed up in two mouthfuls'. In their place there is now an elementary school shoved up in a desert of earth and mud, a secondary school that has never been finished, and, worst of all, a sea of houses piled up without regard for good architecture and good town planning.

Finally, when the documents of the commission became public knowledge and were discussed in the press, instead of penalizing the culprits and attempting to make good the damage, all was settled by a reprieve that let the speculators off with a small penalty. To be precise, in 1973 Signor Nicolò Giammanco was cleared of the accusation of fraud and of having had a private interest in official transactions, and was granted an amnesty on the basis of insufficient evidence. And in 1975, when he had recourse to the court of appeal, his case was judged 'inadmissable', and Signor Giammanco was required to pay only costs.

In this manner, the extraordinary eighteenth-century villas of Bagheria, which are among the most precious heirlooms of Sicily, were stripped of their surroundings and remain there besieged by new houses, numbed and desecrated witnesses to a past that is being wantonly destroyed.

One has only to think of the famous sandstone figures of monsters at the Villa Palagonia. Their originality and their rich extravagance have brought people from all over the world to admire them, photograph them, and write about them. But while once upon a time these Baroque masterpieces of the grotesque stood out elegantly against the sky, today they are swallowed up by a barrage of houses and flats scrambled together in disorderly confusion.

I asked Professor Nino Morreale if the current atmosphere of Bagheria had changed, and he replied: 'Until a magistrate decides to probe the transactions of Bagheria's town council and until everything is entrusted to the goodwill of the few citizens willing to take the situation in hand, there cannot be much hope of change.'

THESE photographs of the villas of Bagheria were probably taken with an old Leica, the same camera as the one my father used; the viewfinder jutting out like a small telescope, the bright metallic body with a dark finish, the small case of pock-marked leather, the focus and exposure which have to be adjusted by hand. The photographs came out well defined and the black and white resolution was clear and sharp like a dry-point etching.

A great photographer with the eyes of a lynx, but the odd thing about my father was that while having so many talents he was never willing to teach me anything. Or perhaps he was, for one day when I was only a little girl of four or five years old, he once taught me the principles of multiplication and addition. But when it came to teaching me to swim he simply threw me into the sea and said 'Swim!' And up in the mountains he said to me 'Walk!' and in the snow which he knew so well, he said 'Go on, go on down!' Only for skiing is there a need for some knowledge of technique and I learned that on my own when I was grown-up, by paying a teacher.

There was a certain reserve between my father and me, something never put into words, which left its mark on our relationship as 'mates'; this had been initiated by him as if there were no differences of age between us, as if one Saturday morning we might together come to a decision to go for a six-hour excursion into the mountains, or go out rowing in the sun for four hours, or for an hour's swim in the icy cold water of the river.

A warning should have been enough and sometimes it was. But even when I imagined my strength to be greater than it was, I would fling myself forward and do my best to keep up with him. Once my mother gave him a slap. He did not return it. He had brought me back from a trip into the mountains which had lasted seven hours in the frost and I had a high temperature and lips that had turned violet, and my feet were quite frozen.

But another time I saved his life. He had to leave early in the morning for a trip into the mountains with some friends. I was ill, I seemed to be delirious. He told his friends to go ahead and he would join them the next day. They went off and were swept away by an avalanche and were all killed.

Between us there was above all a sense of solidarity, a comradeship, a bold independence, an exciting defiance of rules, of ordinary common sense. Like two travelling companions, two sportsmen, two friends for life, we could communicate with each other by a look. Words got in the way, and in fact we spoke little. With me he laughed, played, ran. We were earnest explorers and we got to know the tracks in the middle of the forest. We paddled up the rivers, we faced the perils of the sea but he did not speak; lest words create something limiting and commonplace – at least, if they were spoken out loud; only thought was considered 'noble'. Indeed he wrote, just as his mother used to write – my grandmother, the very beautiful Yoi, half English and half Polish, with whom so many men of her time had fallen in love. It was acceptable to write rather than to talk. This was the silent commandment, never articulated, that was in force between us. I obeyed the rules. But how was I to make use of the love I felt? To write what?

My father's books are those of a scientist and he never ceased to write about ethnology, a science poised between the humanism of antiquity and new technology, which he loved more than anything else, a way of writing that consists of observation and analysis and at the same time is both invention and narration. But I chose pure story-telling, beyond any scientific pretensions unless it were the science of writing itself.

I began by writing poetry which was all about him. And then, with a struggle, my gaze shifted to other faces, other smells, the backs of other necks, other smiles. But with what reluctance! Almost as if the world consisted only of his swaying yet resolute walk, his embarrassed cough, his departure at dawn for a distant future, far away and unknown yet absolutely wonderful.

I went on to read all the books of poetry I could lay my hands on. I remember an edition of Baudelaire with the palest blue cover and a broken back which I stuck together again and again with flour-and-water paste each time it fell apart.

'J'ai longtemps habité sous des spacieux portiques.' But suddenly I remember how this line was constantly on the lips of Alberto, the other father-son, the other travelling companion I have loved in my life.

I remember Quasimodo's translation of Greek lyrics. And the verses of Emily Dickinson which I used to repeat to myself in English under my breath, trying to grasp the secret of their dancing rhythm: pithy, solemn, but also capricious and unpredictable, almost as if in the midst of a procession with tall wax candles and banners, the gentle Emily, always dressed in white, had begun to turn head over heels.

I came to understand that poetry was not so very different from those brain-teasers in geometry, which at first left me with a bitter taste in my mouth. But then while trying to unravel their hidden structures I was seized by an indescribable excitement and happiness. It was the unexpected way of dividing space, the rules governing this division, its subtraction and multiplication beneath my wondering eyes, its inner rhythms matched perfectly together. It was the surprise of this formal organization that brought a lump to my throat. Why can a feeling of joy, elation, and peace arise from one word in conjunction with another word, in such a way that every repetition is different and unpredictable, in spite of their adhering to the conventional rules of language?

I never asked my father anything about writing. It seemed to me that his mere presence, sitting at the table with his back facing the door (which he always insisted must be kept shut), his obstinate insistence on silence, was itself an affirmation of his seriousness and professional discipline.

Those were years in which I confused my dreams with reality. They were precise and lucid dreams, difficult to distinguish from everyday life. They were mostly dreams of travelling, adventure, extraordinary happenings in which I snuggled close to the spirit of little Alice in Wonderland, ready to rush into the dark hole so as to discover something new and fascinating. I also dreamed of flying. As I suffered from giddiness, my flight from one roof to another like a breathless swallow filled me with shivers of fear and pleasure.

I dreamed that my father, on one of the rare times he returned to Bagheria, took me with him into the mouth of Pinnochio's whale. There we read books together and drank wine sitting at a table that jerked up and down on the rasping tongue of the whale, while from outside the sea spray splashed in over us. This scene came from a book by Collodi and I enjoyed its descriptions of the sea, of domestic life and family customs, even if the situation inside the belly of the whale was decidedly implausible. In some way I wished my father was my son, so that I could have kept him shut inside my belly instead of seeing him always going off to far-away places that were beyond my imagination.

'IN the year 1400, there was considerable development of agriculture in Bagheria,' writes that diligent historian Girgenti.

There was an expansion in the cultivation of olives, vineyards, and sugar cane. In 1468 Pietro Speciale obtained the barony of Ficarazzi from the king. Together with Ludovico Del Campo and Umbertino Imperatore he began the cultivation of sugar cane in the valley of the river Eleuterio where it could be irrigated, and in addition they started a sugar cane enterprise in the castle, also commissioned by the same Speciale.

That's where the taste for *sfizi*, the sugared sweets found in Bagheria, originated. The art of making them was preserved for centuries by the nuns. And *trionfi di gola* was talked about at length in the Japanese concentration camp. To my childish imagination it seemed like one of the marvels of a lost paradise. 'A green hillock made of pistachio jelly mingled with candied orange, sweet ricotta, raisins and pieces of chocolate.' When my mother described it she was unable to move her legs from beriberi, a disease of malnutrition. But she had not lost the courage with which she faced the 'hunger strikes', or her turn at night to listen secretly to the guard's radio. 'It melts in your mouth like a cloud giving off an intense and overwhelming perfume. It is like eating a mountain landscape with all its woods, its rivers, its meadows; a landscape rendered light and friable by clouds of cotton wool that enclose it and transform it from being a joy to the eyes to becoming a joy to the tongue. You hold your breath and feel blessed by this extraordinary morsel of sugar, a world suspended on your tongue like a most precious gift from the gods. But of course you can't eat more than a spoonful; if you did you would become terribly sick.'

They still make exquisite ices in Bagheria today: little chocolate flowers filled with soft ice-cream scented with jasmine, mint, strawberries, or coconut, as well as the more traditional melon ice, which is not a real ice-cream but a jelly of watermelon the colour of coral speckled with grains of chocolate. And words are inadequate to describe the *gelato di campagna*, a kind of delicately coloured sugared nougat, with the flavour of pistachio blended with almonds and vanilla.

The last time I ate the sweet cakes of Bagheria was when I visited my Aunt Saretta at the Villa Valguarnera. Later on she died, leaving the villa and all the estate to the Jesuits, to the great dismay of her relations who in fact contested the will. The Jesuits very sensibly thought that such a monumental villa would be hard to maintain, and they washed their hands of it. Meanwhile, thieves broke in and took everything, even the garden statues.

Nothing was left for my mother, even though she was the daughter of the eldest of the Alliata brothers, because my grandmother Sonia had sold up everything before she died. When she was eighty she entered into a contract with Aunt Saretta: a life annuity in return for her share of the villa after her death. And when she died Aunt Saretta held on to everything.

Now I'm glad to have visited Aunt Saretta for the last time a short while before she died. Today I can no longer go into the old family home. When I saw it last all the furniture and pictures that were later stolen were still there, including the portrait of Marianna, which would be so important to my later work as a writer.

I had telephoned Aunt Saretta to ask whether I could see her. And she, reluctantly, had said, 'Come if you really want to.' But I knew she did not like me. Strictly Catholic, monarchist and conservative, she saw me as a spurious product of the family, a degenerate branch, a malign excrescence that if it could not be exterminated could at least be ignored.

I went there with a friend from my childhood who had stayed with us during those first years when we were living in the stables on our return from Japan. The iron gate with the Alliata and Valguarnera coat of arms was shut. I tried to hail somebody but the porter's lodge was empty. I pushed against the bottom part of the gate and it yielded. I entered the drive. The caretaker's lodge was still there, dark and bolted.

When I was small, that gate was always open, and on the threshold the good and generous Innocenza would be sitting like a *parca buona*, one of those ancient divinities intent on sewing up the threads of life, her fat shapeless body, her yellow broken teeth, a smile always on her lips and a pair of wire-framed glasses tied behind her ears with a piece of string. I can still remember her apron with its smell of fried fish, fresh basil, soap and tomato purée.

Innocenza spent all day sewing and keeping an eye on the gate. When someone arrived, she would ask what they wanted but without the inquisitorial attitude of so many porters. She would put her hand to her forehead as if to shield herself from the sun, even though it never shone on the threshold because it was shielded by a sloping roof, and she would smile and nod her head as a sign of assent. If a car arrived, she would get up laboriously, put down her sewing and go to push open the two heavy iron grilles with all the weight of her body.

I had not thought of her for years, but on opening the gate I was suddenly struck by her absence. She had been a benign presence, a *parca buona* whom I knew had sewn and resewn the threads of my destiny, spinning them, separating them, knotting them to make them happy and long-lasting. I used to sense her indulgent look at my back as I set off for school early in the day. I knew I could face a whole morning of boredom with the help of that look, which I carried on my back like a protective hump. When I returned all excited around two o'clock, I would bring her a bag of roasted chickpeas, with their cheerful savour of the night, out of which she would fish a few and leave the rest for me.

She knew all the village gossip but she was never malicious, indeed she tried to remedy all the jealousies and all the envies, putting in a few words here, a kindly hint there. She was always ready to see good emerge from evil, like a ripe juicy cactus fruit emerging from its thorny sword-shaped leaves powdered with the dust of communal living.

It was she who told me of Fila who had got herself pregnant at fifteen by her brother-in-law and of how her brothers had decided in cold blood to kill him immediately in revenge for his having taken her.

And she told me too of a little boy of eleven who had seen something he should not have seen and who one morning had been taken, bound, blinded with a knife used to cut pigs' throats, and then sent home tied up like a sausage and dripping with blood.

And of another, Don Peppinuzzu, the handsome one, who had said something he should not have said and so was battered to death. Then they cut off his balls and put them in his mouth. His mother had found him like that beneath a mulberry tree as she went to the fields in the morning.

At that time the mafia was never spoken about. Everybody knew that an evil force existed, which was capable of imposing its will with the knife or the gun. But who wielded the knife or who shouldered the gun was difficult to say. Moreover, for anyone who did know, it was wiser to pretend never to have known. Those who were influential in the village, the men who paraded on the pavements in tight pyjama jackets wearing wide-brimmed hats, denied the existence of any mafia. And when they pronounced the word they pursed their lips as if about to spit. They waved their hands and said with a snigger, 'Tall stories, all tourist stuff.' And with that the village closed in on its everyday affairs made up of abuses, suffering, wrongs endured in silence, things hushed up and never spoken of, as if it were the happiest place in the world.

Sometimes Innocenza deposited her sewing on the table, dragged her chair on to the end of the terrace and started to delouse her niece Carmelina, crushing the lice with professional skill between the nails of both thumbs. And if a car or a carriage arrived, she would leave her niece and go to open the gate with her bloodstained fingers, her ready smile, and that avid curious look of the old caretaker who watches whoever enters or leaves life or death by night or by day.

Innocenza is no more. She was already old when I was ten and I imagine she must be dead. In her place there is a bolted door. I try to push it. It yields under my hand and opens on to black emptiness. There, after groping down two steps, I find myself in front of an enormous dresser of stained wood in which are arranged an array of plates with floral patterns and long-stemmed glasses, which had been used only for important occasions such as a wedding or a confirmation. Between the glass front and the wooden edge of the dresser photographs have been inserted; one of a son killed in the war; one of the mother, a small slender figure with the eyes of a hawk. Inside an oval mount such as the local photographer used to have, one of a daughter who was married only a short time ago.

M Y childhood friend Bice Pasqualino and I go on foot along the drive that leads up to the villa, leaving the car outside the gate. The drive runs uphill, first going straight and then suddenly curving round and passing below a terrace supported by high arches; it continues between two rows of tamarisks, between which rises a stunted sapling, a so-called *scopazzo*, or broom tree.

The big oleanders, the colour of melting sunrise, which I used to see every morning as I went to school, have vanished; I don't know why. But everything has been obliterated through indifference and neglect.

And it is here that after walking for another hundred yards, one lifts one's eyes and suddenly finds oneself in front of the Villa Valguarnera in all its beauty; a central façade on two floors with a succession of windows, some real and some blind, that flow with a movement both severe and playful. From the centre two wings open out to form a perfect semicircle. Originally, in the early years of the eighteenth century, at the time when Marianna Valguarnera had transformed the hunting lodge of her father into a villa, the two wings had been built with arches which followed an insistent yet delicate rhythm. Later on, these arches were walled up to form stables and hen houses, to be followed eventually by flats and garages.

In the centre of the villa is an elegant curved staircase spreading into an arc and rising up to the first floor to give a gracious lightness and plasticity to the entire façade. The two side wings enclose a courtyard whose perfect symmetry brings to mind the shape of a concert hall. The proportions are of a studied and pleasing harmony, revealing a taste for the theatrical and for geometric design that was typical of the Age of Enlightenment. Even if, in Sicily, the lights were always veiled and dimmed with filigree, which softened their intensity in the pursuit of beauty and discernment.

Many of the windows giving on to the two wings are blind, painted on the walls in the style of baroque *trompe-l'oeil*, with their shutters and with contemplative figures looking out of half-open window frames. All this is none other than a delight in the pleasure of representation, as if to imply that the outside of a house invents the inside – perhaps not in fact, perhaps only in the imagination, but more fascinating and more realistic than what is on the other side of the walls – a reality that may be only fanciful but one with greater substance than what is actually there, impoverished as it is by the usual banality of everyday life, yet confirming that every representation contains in itself internal truths which transcend outward truth. From this comes that artful elegance, that hint of attraction to disquieting changes, to extravagant ideas, to impossible dreams.

And here she is in an oval-shaped frame, Marianna Alliata Valguarnera, in an idealized pose, half goddess and half scholar, wrapped in the folds of a sumptuous dress. The portrait is cracked right down its length. It was said in the family that the damage was done by Queen Maria Louisa, wife of King Ferdinand of Bourbon, who tried to break it when she came to spend a few days at the villa during her exile from Naples.

That despairing city had made its own little 'Jacobin Revolution' and put in place of its patron Saint Gennaro a tree of freedom festooned with French and Italian flags waving in the sunshine. I have often though about this Jacobin Naples and written about it to try and create a play. Central character: Eleonora Fonseca Pimental, who was first of all librarian to Queen Carolina and then became a rabid Jacobin who wrote articles in the *Monitore* to incite the crowds to revolt against the Bourbons and arranged street meetings, nonchalantly pulling up her skirt above her small lacquered slippers and speaking in dialect so that everyone would be able to understand her.

Eleonora the Jacobin was for a long time the confidante of Queen Carolina, who herself was for a while a confidante of one of my distant forebears. She lived in the villa to which I am now returning with my burden of curiosity and inquisitiveness, having written a play about that same librarian, who was hanged in the Piazza della Vicaria.

Oh Lady Leonora you used to sing on high,
Now you dance in the market place swinging in the sky.
Long live His Holiness who sent the little cannons in
To drive away those Jacobins.

Along the roof of the Villa Valguarnera rise statues that stand out in graceful theatrical poses against the clear silken sky. Cupids armed with arrows, Venuses larger than life-size,

Neptunes, Centaurs, all of whom seen from the courtyard take on a look of stillness and an almost divine protection.

As we make our way towards the stairs, a door opens and Aunt Saretta appears, her skin mottled with brown blotches, a necklace of amber beads as large as walnuts round her emaciated neck, and a cold, detached but polite smile on her painted red lips. Seeing her, one would not have thought she could be so devout as to leave her whole estate to the Jesuits.

'She has nothing of the Alliatas about her.' The thought comes to me almost as if I had suddenly developed an interest in issues of kinship which I have always despised. For years, I have absolutely erased such questions from my life, those flights of fancy about relationships, considering them to be so alien that I have never felt any desire to take account of them. I was ashamed of belonging through my mother to such an ancient and noble family. Could she really have come from them, from one of those great families that were so avaricious, hypocritical and rapacious, the root of so many of Sicily's misfortunes? I hated their atavistic inability to change, to see the truth, to understand other people, to cease being so aloof, to act with humility. The idea of sharing anything with them, even if it were only an involuntary resemblance, repelled me.

Yet my grandfather was so far removed from the stereotype of an arrogant and presumptuous nobleman that I realized I had done him an injustice, probably due to the ideological loves of my youth. It is always short-sighted and limiting to pigeon-hole people, whether it is into a class or a sex. It can be foolish not to take into account that some things are unpredictable. Just as foolish is the idea of a world of equals without losers, without personal histories, without unique events and the footprints of interior journeys which have no destination and no end in view.

'For many years Enrico di Salaparuta was interested in theosophy and anthroposophy,' my sister Toni wrote in her delightful portrait of my grandfather (which can be found in the preface to a little book of thoughts and aphorisms published by Semar).

He had travelled in Switzerland and Holland, he had managed to get hold of all the standard works, and had discussed them with his cosmopolitan Sicilian friend Tom Virzi and other friends who all used to meet together in groups. To get an impression of how comprehensive the libraries of these Sicilians were, it is worth remembering that all the best known works of Rudolf Steiner, Annie Besant and Allen Kardec were published in Catania and Palermo between 1900 and 1930.

Simple in his dress, his manner and his speech, inspired by liberal and democratic ideas, Enrico was much loved. Paradoxically, although opposed to any kind of idealism, at the end of his life in Casteldaccia he was thought of as a saint. And this was not so much for his qualities as a worshipper of nature, a vegetarian and a pacifist opposed to any form of clerical or authoritarian ideas, but rather by the example he gave through the simplicity and wisdom with which he conducted his everyday life.

Aunt Saretta came from a family of the Calabrian nobility and she had married the son of one of Enrico's brothers. She had a sister who married another uncle from the Alliata family. So two brothers married two sisters. The first did not have any children, the second had a daughter who grew up determined to make use of her intellect. Indeed she writes courageously and passionately today about the Arab world. But there were almost no sons – as if great families which only a few generations ago were rich in both male and female descendants were now possessed by a dark drive for self-extinction.

I saw Grandfather Enrico, who was already dying, when we came back from Japan. I do not remember much of him, except for his bed in the half-light, and the fresh smell of flowers mixed with the smell of medicines, two very gentle, tired, half-closed eyes. Instead, I enjoyed looking at a photograph of him my mother had given me, when he was twenty years old and wearing fancy dress. It was the costume of a nobleman of the eighteenth century with damask knee-breeches and a redingote gleaming with sumptuous embroidery; at the neck a jabot flashing delicate lace; on his head a tricorn hat with white feathers; on his feet light shoes ornamented with silver buckles; through an opening in his jacket at the waist, a little sword of which only the hilt of beaten metal was visible; beneath his feet a carpet with pastoral designs and behind, a window with embroidered curtains.

Thus attired, Grandfather Enrico raises his eyes to gaze up at the camera with the look of someone who knows how good-looking he is but does not take it too seriously. From the restricted view that can be seen through the window it looks as if it were taken at the Villa Valguarnera.

At the villa there was a theatre and it was a family tradition to put on musical and theatrical events. Aunt Felicita, a sister of Grandfather Enrico, played the violin, Enrico sang, his wife Sonia had a magnificent soprano voice, and Aunt Amelia played the piano. All this took place in Bagheria towards the end of the last century.

In the photograph, Grandfather Enrico wears his hair long, with thick curls falling down to his shoulders. Hair that my mother inherited from him, and which I, in my turn, have inherited from her; hair that tends to grow all over the place, tangled in reckless disorder. 'Hair like a savage', as it used to be called by a teacher at the boarding school in Florence where I was incarcerated for three long years after the war in order to learn how to behave like a 'well-brought-up young lady'. For this teacher with her long white fingers everything had to be 'just so', from one's stockings to the ends of one's hair. Mine was scraped back, curry-combed, and held tight in two plaits that dangled mortified and insipid on each side of my ears.

Grandfather Enrico's eyes were exactly like my mother's, large and blue, a little lost and dreamy. They were the eyes of someone accustomed to the privileges of his world which he had cheerfully come to hold in contempt and to detest. His nose was also similar to my mother's; straight, severe, with an almost perceptible bump in the middle, the two wings of the nostrils soft and sensual; two sensitive nostrils with something about them of a dog that can sniff out people and recognize things by their smell. His mouth had large well-defined lips, but these I have not inherited from my mother. My mouth is small, with blurred edges and something slack and formless about it. Now it is also bitter and withered, ready to dissolve into a submissive disconsolate smile.

A smile that springs out of wells of anxiety. I have hated my submissiveness as a sign of insecurity. A smile, mine, giving in to anyone who can dissolve me with a look of annoyance, as my father used to do sometimes, so taken up was he with his own affairs, his unshackled thoughts, and his passion for sport and for travelling the world. A propitiatory smile towards that dark adult world whose gods seem to have been angered at my birth and to have played dangerously with my future.

They stay to watch, these inscrutable divinities, how far my endurance can stretch. I am always in suspense, hovering between a profound fear that disturbs me without reason, and an icy calm that sustains me in the face of danger. They stay high above me, roosting like golden doves. Great gods, descending to search for anyone who will offer them hospitality.

But they did not find anybody willing to have them in their home. So they encamped near the one with the most worn shoes, the most unfortunate of all creatures, Shen-Te, that accommodating spirit of She-tzuan, as Brecht recounts, who having generously invited guests to her house, had been given a tobacco shop as a gift. There she was found by various impoverished relations and friends who set out to divide up her good fortune to such an extent that they reduced her to bankruptcy. And in a moment of good sense she created her double, Shui-Ta, who helped her extricate herself from this awkward situation. I ask myself when shall I learn to divide myself in two as successfully as the good soul of She-tzuan.

I believe I have inherited this urge to accommodate other people from the Alliata side of the family. In fact, looking back, I realize that my grandparents, uncles, great-uncles, great-grandfathers and great-grandmothers were all gentle and pacific people who tended to get married to men and women of an authoritarian character who ended by trampling them underfoot, while they took refuge in their dreams.

ACCORDING to my Aunt Felicita in her delightful book, *Memories from the Past*, which for years I contemptuously put aside, my great-grandparents were aristocrats of the old school, ponderous, gentle, conservative. Yet a minor rebellion crept into their seigneurial old age.

My father lived for much of the time at Casteldaccia so as to keep in touch with his farms and vineyards. Casteldaccia is the village where the wine called Corvo di Sala Paruta was, and still is, made. (It was first created and named by the father of Grandfather Enrico.) In the evening he and my grandmother used to receive important people from the neighbourhood, all Bourbon informers, and my grandmother would sing and play the piano in front of the assembled guests. But inside the piano they had hidden a store of arms and ammunition. Thus they lived happily in the midst of danger.

Aunt Felicita never got married. It was said in the family that the reason was that she wanted to remain faithful to her betrothed who, years before, had gone down with his ship on the high seas.

I have a copy of a photograph of her in eighteenth-century fancy dress – perhaps because Villa Valguarnera was built in that century, perhaps because the time of the greatest splendour of the Alliata family had coincided with the building of the villa, and so all the fancy dress was related to the century of wigs and tricorn hats, pigtails and little swords, to the Marina Theatre, to the music of Scarlatti and the poetry of Metastasio.

My grandfather had three sisters: Amalia, who was the most beautiful and of whom there is a photograph in Aunt Felicita's book, dressed for some unknown reason as a mediaeval lady; Maria, the second sister, who was a good viola player; and Felicita, who was an accomplished violinist. Together they were part of a small youth orchestra that played in the big Massimo Theatre in Palermo 'before royalty', as vouched for by Aunt Felicita, 'with Master Giuseppe Mulé Lo Monaco Sgadari who was the leading spirit of the evening'. I too had a chance of knowing Giuseppe Lo Monaco Sgadari, called Beppuzzu. He must have been very young at the time of the musical evenings at the Massimo Theatre. The year when the Alliata sisters played there was 1906. When I knew him, at the end of the 1950s, he kept a sumptuous table in his beautiful house close to the harbour at Palermo. But, now I come to think about it, he must have been the son because he was not so very old when I knew him.

The Beppuzzo whom I knew was renowned for his library and for his collection of gramophone records. It was said that he had more than ten thousand. His house was filled with the ablest young people from all over the town, and he was happy to invite them for lunch and supper, provided they were young and gifted and loved books and could shift comfortably from Saint Augustine to Proust, from Thomas Mann to Adorno. Adrian Leverkühn was one of his idols and everybody was expected to have experienced the acidulous quality of his phenomenal erudition in music and philosophy.

His collection of 78 r.p.m. records was famed throughout the city and, after supper, one could sit discussing great ideas and the masterpieces of literature, or alternatively recline on brocade-covered sofas listening to Mozart and Wagner. In general, opera was considered 'vulgar', and Verdi seen as a 'band leader'. Only Mozart was tolerated as the inventor of opera, and to some extent Wagner. Puccini was seen as sentimental, 'something for the servant's hall'. The music most appreciated and analysed was that of quartets and he would talk for hours about resonance, musical composition, melody, rhythm, timbre and structure.

From time to time some girl, a friend of one of the young men, would be tolerated at a musical evening, and even for a supper of stuffed swordfish and chocolate mousse. One of them was myself, even though I was a complete ignoramus about music. But I was not behind anyone in reading. I had devoured before they had *The Magic Mountain* and *Joseph and his Brethren* in the classical Medusa edition, with its green paper cover with a calf's head and two little wings. And I knew who Becky Sharp and Nastasya Filippovna were. I had taken to heart the fate of Madame Bovary and I could repeat by heart the thoughts of Bezuchov. But I was very shy and I never imagined that I would be able to say out loud in public what I was thinking to myself.

Moreover, along with other things, my critical faculties had been little developed. I could have the most complicated theories but I had no idea how to explain the whys and wherefores of the excitement I got from them.

I listened fascinated to old Beppuzzo, who held court sunk into a rickety armchair, sometimes dressed informally in velvet trousers and a silk housecoat, the lapels covered in snuff that he sniffed up his nose, laying the powder on the back of his hand like they used to do in the time of his great-grandparents. Around him were gathered the most gifted young men of Palermo: the erudite Francesco, the handsome Ernesto, the logical Giuseppe, the quick-witted Gio with that provocative quiff of hair falling over his forehead, the seductive Nino who used to quote Molière, Antonio the imaginative puppeteer. They were all young men with great hopes for the future who made a religion of intelligence and fed off only the very choicest things, such as music and poetry.

We played with the 'sublime', and somehow managed to convince ourselves we were living in a golden age which, leaping over the intervening blind alleys, harked back to the exclusive circle of Greek philosophers; those great promenaders of the Agora of philosophy with Socrates and his devoted followers. The horrors of daily existence – poverty, political intrigues, the brutality of smalltime murders – were all banished outside the door. One went in, taking off one's shoes as in a temple of delight and learning, a most chaste delight that was entirely satisfied by divine music, exquisite dishes, and an ambience of words with quotations from Greek and Latin.

When Beppuzzo Lo Monaco died, he left 'a little something' to each of the young people who used to commune with him over a plate of *pasta con le sarde* and a soufflé of orange and vanilla.

On one occasion I invited them all to Bagheria, to a party at the Villa Valguarnera; I think it was on my birthday. There was a full moon and I had made myself a new milk-white dress.

I could feel its taste on my tongue, just as when I was a child I used to judge dresses by the tastes they aroused in me.

Some of the guests never turned up; perhaps I had not known how to invite them properly. Others arrived late, when the moon was already going down in the sky and the food was getting cold. Then an unexpected wind got up and sent the table napkins flying and swept away the plates and tablecloths. Finally, somebody overturned a small cup of coffee, ruining my beautiful white dress forever. Later, I seem to remember, someone in the family dyed it dark brown so that it would not be thrown away. Only thus could the coffee stain be made invisible. But the taste of that dark brown dress was cloying and disagreeable. I never wore it again.

Rereading the book by Aunt Felicita, I can see how the gossip that circulated about her in the family was attributed by her to another Felicita, or Felice, sister of her grandfather Edoardo. 'Aunt Felice, as they called her, was a Canoness of Bavaria', Aunt Felicita tells us.

The King of Bavaria at that time was, I think, Maximillian II and when he came to Palermo, being a friend of the family, he came to visit her on the top floor of the house where she resided. My father, then only a child, was amazed to see the King coming up the big staircase accompanied by two servants carrying lighted torches. The cross belonging to the Canoness, in blue and white enamel with an image of the Madonna, and her blue and white scarf were stolen with all the investiture in 1914.

Aunt Felice was not beautiful like the other sisters but she was very attractive, and she had the aquiline nose of the family. She was pleasant and kindly and it seems she had many admirers. But she refused all of them, because she grieved so much for the death of her betrothed, and in consequence she became a nun. One day, among her things, I found a daguerrotype in a leather case representing a handsome young man with side whiskers and curls over his ears, a typical hairstyle, together with a letter. . . . I knew that he had been an officer in the French Navy and had perished when his ship went down. In the letter the parents wrote to tell his betrothed of this misfortune and to send her a ring of his.

This aunt, just like her great-niece of the same name, painted flowers. *Le langage des fleurs*: 'There are forty-four engravings incised on copper that concentrate on the same image. In each is a minute figure and a saying appropriate to every sentimental feeling of the Romantic period.'

The phrases were the kind that said *Di te noi*, 'from us to you'. Others said 'She is flighty', or spoke of 'Hope in time'. And two intertwined hands held a piece of red embroidery: 'In life, in death'. A sword and an olive branch were placed next to the word 'Choose'. 'They make me smile,' commented Aunt Felicita benevolently, 'and I leave it to the girls of today to make fun of them.'

Among 'the girls of today' was my mother, blonde and resplendent, intolerant of all maternal restrictions and contemptuous of any 'great marriage' the family tried to impose on her. In fact, abandoning all the traditions of the Sicilian nobility, she went off on her own to Florence where she met my father, a cheerful, brusque young man, rebellious and solitary, athletic and restless, introverted and unpredictable. They got married immediately, without a penny, and went to live at Fiesole in a room at the top of a tower, eating boiled potatoes and boiled eggs.

The eyes of both the Maraini and the Alliata families closed in disgust at the sight of these two presumptuous young people who thought they could throw the whole of the past out through the window and go off, naked and alone, towards the uncertainties of the future as if nothing mattered, without even a guilty conscience.

Strange, the family geometry that opens the past like a fan. Two parents, four grandparents, eight great-grandparents and so on. While towards the future there are no offspring; the family has come to a halt with me. Except for my one son, much wanted and longed for, who died shortly before birth, attempting to drag me with him. So I made the decision that what I would take into the future would be the characters in my novels, sons and daughters with strong legs able to walk long distances.

Aunt Felicita also came to a full stop. She did not wish to procreate. And the family attributed to her the same fate as that of her great-aunt, the Canoness of Bavaria: a betrothed drowned at sea, a vow of chastity kept until death. The strange destiny of a name – Felicita – which promises much happiness and which wastes away in a long and tragic solitude.

AUNT Saretta asks me why I want so much to visit the villa which was my childhood home. 'To write about it,' I say. She gives me an incredulous look. In her aristocratic head I could only have come to ferret out who knows what secrets to use in 'lurid articles against the nobility'. This much is clear from the way she tells me sternly 'not to take photographs of any kind whatsoever'. And when she lets me into the hall cluttered with climbing plants, she makes sure I do not have a tape-recorder hidden on me. She treats me as though I am a newspaper reporter on the lookout for scandal.

'And who is this woman?' she asks suspiciously, expecting me to have arrived from Rome with some unknown accomplice in my dangerous journalistic exploits. Then she recognizes Bice, daughter of a well-known doctor in Palermo, married to someone as nobly born as herself, and she calms down. Bice, the calmest and gentlest person in the world, smiles affectionately, incapable as she is of feeling antipathy towards anyone.

And Aunt Saretta becomes quite loquacious. She tells us about the recent restorations. 'The cupid on the left-hand side of the roof has lost a foot . . . then the burglars got in for the fourth time this year and went off with the rest of the silver. . . . Luckily after having loaded up the garden statues they got scared by something, I don't know what, and they went off leaving the loot behind. But the statues had fallen to the ground and their heads got broken off their bodies.'

It seems like a symbol of the island: its beauty snatched away, ravished twice, thrice, a hundred times, the head broken off from the body and a stony silence masking every torment in an elegant attempt to portray the loss of self shut away in a distrust without escape, a stranger unknown to oneself, prey to a grief that has no voice.

Meanwhile we come to the room that had once belonged to my grandmother. As we struggle to open the shutters which have been closed for a long time, the light floods in like water over the parched walls. The floor, with its old faded carpets, seems to be bathed in a liquid dust that shimmers gently, sending billions of golden motes into the air.

My eyes look for the piano which used to stand against the wall at the end of the room and on which my grandmother used to play and sing. It is still there. The burglars have spared it. They must have judged it to be completely worthless with its worm-eaten wood, its yellowing keys and its missing strings. Above it are still the photograph frames I had always seen there, hanging a little askew. Only the silver ones have disappeared; the others, made of glass, china or wood, are still in their place.

There is one of Aunt Felicita as a young woman, a large peaked brigand's cap rammed down on her head; the same mouth as my grandfather and my mother. The mouth that bent over me in a Japanese room humming the tender motif from *Madame Butterfly*. Until she came to me I was unable to get to sleep. I would lie thinking of her being kidnapped. My mother was so beautiful that anyone might want to take her away, I used to think, turning over and over in my bed. The idea that by growing up I could be causing my mother to grow old used to give me terrible fits of guilt. I tried to stop growing so that she would stop getting old. If only I were able to halt this hurrying rabbit with a fob watch always in its hand, everything would be all right and my mother, with her lovely geranium mouth, would continue eternally to bend over me, telling me the story of the three pomegranates. 'Once more, mama!' The word 'mama' came from the Spanish; we never used 'mamma' or 'mother' in our family, just as we never used childish words like 'bum' or 'thingy', etc. For us the female genitals were *cin-cin* and the male genitals *cimbo*, Japanese words which were used exclusively for the male and female genitals of children. As for the bottom, it was called *jotito*, as in Spanish.

'But I've already told you the story of the three pomegranates.'

'But I want it again, I want it again!'

'Then, once upon a time there was a king who had three daughters. . . .'

In another photograph all five of us are there; my father with his Mongolian good looks, shut away in seductive silence, my mother in an Ingrid Bergman pose, with a rosy glow in her cheeks and stars in her eyes, me with the smocking on my dress that mingled green and yellow flowers in a bluish flicker and titillated my palate. It was a time when I would put on a dress and immediately become aware of its taste – something I can still remember by shutting my eyes. It would come out of my throat like a faint cloud. They were delicious tastes:

70

ripe melon, dry grass, harvested wheat, dried egg, curdled milk, stewed cherries, half-open lilies, sour medlars, holly, daisies. . . .

My sister Yuki has a high forehead of a very tender delicate whiteness, and the same almond-shaped eyes as my father: dark, intense, obstinate – the Maraini eyes. And the youngest, Toni, has a round freckled face, a gap between her front teeth that makes her look a little comic, already lost behind her gentle silent brooding.

There is a moment in the history of every family when it sees itself as happy, even if this is not actually so. But one carries it, written on one's face: I am a family only recently created, in my fullness and in my neediness. I am food for the eyes of others, I am the earthly flesh that imitates the divine flesh, I am the family in all its earthly bliss. It was this kind of happiness that was imprinted on the photograph, bursting out of the eyes, the clothes, the sense of unity, the wondering, the searching, the venturing, the sniffing that we have in common with animals.

Afterwards, I don't know how, everything broke up and started to disintegrate. The rose has given the best of itself; now the petals fall one by one, and it looks more like a rotten tooth than a flower. The scent is the last thing to go, that light scent of sleeping bodies, of youthful and tender breath, the perfume that helps to create the perfection of the family as it comes into being.

It is terrible to find oneself grown-up, no longer in that paradise of sensations and smells, and to understand how that happiness has only been preserved in a few photographs. The shock of finding in one's nostrils those smells of maternal beds and to know they have been lost forever.

Another photograph shows my Grandmother Sonia as a young woman: a broad face with prominent cheekbones. She was dark, with the whitest of skins, black eyebrows and black hair that came from her native country, Chile. She used to say she had native Indian blood in her veins.

Her eyes were large and shining, while her smile was hard and arrogant.

One of these eyes dominated her bedroom, enlarged a hundred times: a fetish, a sign of the hereafter such as I have seen hanging in smoky rooms in Guatemalan villages. It is the eye of a malevolent god to whom you must be forever offering gifts, otherwise your house will be set on fire or you will die of consumption.

Each eyelash a little stick, the skin of the eyelids bleached white, shining like the scales of a fish. That eye followed me all over the house, searching and mocking, all around it a kind of semi-darkness that evoked infernal shades and volcanic frowns. I knew how these shadows came into existence: every morning I would see her rubbing burnt cork round her eyes.

I never saw my Grandmother Sonia cry. Not even when my grandfather died. She outlived him for almost thirty years, the beautiful girl from Chile who at eighty was still unable to speak Italian properly. She constructed her sentences according to the rhythm and logic of the Spanish language. She used to say *el uomo* and did not distinguish between *cappello* (hat) and *capello* (hair). She would say, 'Esci così, en cuerpo?', meaning that someone was not wearing a *capotto*, an overcoat.

She came from Chile at the end of the last century with her father, who was an ambassador, and she studied the piano and singing in Paris. She had a beautiful soprano voice and a theatrical temperament, so much so that all her teachers encouraged her to make a career out of singing. But it was not a profession for girls of good family and her father forbade it. Instead, he suddenly proposed a 'good' marriage to an Argentinian landowner. But she refused and at eighteen ran away from home to go and 'make songs', as she put it. She landed up in Milan, where she came to know Caruso who got her started at the school of La Scala. A photograph of Caruso with an inscription to the 'clever and beautiful Sonia' was well known in the family. Even the famous music publisher

Ricordi had judged her to have exceptional talent as an opera singer.

However, her father Ortuzar had no intention of yielding. He went and fetched her from Milan and brought her back to Paris. And from Paris she escaped once more. She showed a great tenacity and a great love for the art of singing.

In an unrestrained contest of wills her father Ortuzar came back to fetch her. He found her hiding in a friend's house and brought her home to France for the second time. But this time he shut her up in her room, swearing he would never let her out except to get married. Then, faced with the violence of her reaction, he took fright. Exactly what these violent reactions were is not recorded. I imagine her throwing herself on the floor as she was later prone to do even after she was married, shrieking, shouting, and contorting herself in a fit of nervous hysteria. In the end her father took her back to Milan so that she could continue to study, but under his strict surveillance.

It was then that Sonia got acquainted with the handsome blue-eyed Sicilian who was my grandfather Enrico, and fell in love with him. Or perhaps he fell in love with her, so passionate, so extrovert, so theatrical, while he was shy, silent, gentle and ironic.

However, not even the young Enrico could tolerate his wife being an opera singer, and he took her back with him to his great house in Palermo where she soon became pregnant. Not being allowed to become a singer was the consequence of love and was not so harsh and upsetting as when her father had prohibited it. While she could not accept parental authority she was able to accept the restraining love of a good-looking husband.

Enrico had to promise her that she would have permission to go on singing. And he kept his word – only, it was understood, for charity evenings and other rare occasions, without any hope of it as a profession, but solely for the pleasure of doing it.

Innocenza used to say 'The duchess is doing an opera,' whenever she heard her screaming at her husband. As a properly brought-up girl of the nineteenth century, she could never ask directly for anything she wanted but would try to get it by using her powers of seduction. If this failed she would make a scene that ended with her rolling on the floor in convulsions.

Recently, my mother has explained what a very frustrated woman my grandmother was. She never liked Sicily, and she was never happy in her marriage in spite of the fact that my grandfather was a kindly and gentle husband. All her life she regretted not being on the stage and being unable to devote herself to music in the way she wanted.

All this was made worse when she lost her only son through a streptococcal infection being diagnosed too late. And even worse by her husband spending more and more time away at Casteldaccia looking after his vineyards or at Valguarnera seeing to his lemon and his carob trees. She stayed on her own in the big mansion in the Piazza Bologni leading a social life. She went to dinner and supper parties, attended the opera, played cards, and was admired by all the most ardent men about town.

When I first knew her she still had a smooth round face, but her body was fat and flabby. Yet she dressed with care in a style that was a little too flashy: big organdie skirts, close-fitting bodices, shoes of the same colour as her silk blouse. In the evening she made much use of sequins and fringes, with an elegance that was reminiscent of the theatre, at times even of the circus.

Two or three times I found myself having to sleep with her in the big bed lacquered with white and gold on the top floor of the Villa Valguarnera. I used to experience a shiver of terror lest even my foot should touch her. From her body emanated a heat that spread between the sheets like a stove, and for some reason this heat was absolutely hateful to me. It was as if I were there with this stove-body in order to remind me of the laws of heredity. I had a horror of resembling her. Fortunately, I have inherited nothing from her except for a certain heaviness in my arms and a good timbre of voice.

I looked furtively in my mother for characteristics that might have passed from one generation to the next. My mother, luckily, inherited almost everything from her father: the colour of her hair, the clarity of her blue eyes. And she has transmitted them to me. She always refused to learn to sing or to play the piano, even though her voice is tender and serene, while that of my grandmother was painfully shrill. My grandmother never read a book and was suspicious of anyone who had their nose in one. She herself was 'as ignorant as a nanny-goat'.

My dislike of Grandmother Sonia mirrored my mother's. She never loved her. Nor did Aunt Orietta, although she and her mother looked very alike. They were both dark, with big languorous eyes encircled by a halo of deep shadow, evoking the thought of unforgettable passions and promises of melting tenderness. Since then, I have come to realize how much Grandmother Sonia was afraid that the beauty of her daughters might grow to be greater than her own – much more than she feared getting old herself. 'She forced us to cover up our breasts when we were fifteen,' my mother told me. 'She used to dress us like children, we were re-legated to the servants' quarters and never introduced to guests.'

Because she had only studied the piano and the rudiments of foreign languages as was then customary for girls, my grandmother had no other interests beyond her voice and her sombre beauty. Like many of her contemporaries she thought relationships between people were resolved through either seduction or hatred. There could be no half measures. All emotions were expressed visibly through her body: fainting fits, enticing smiles, the innuendo of bare arms; there was nothing else. Words were of no use to her and reason even less.

All this resulted in isolating her. Her husband avoided her, her daughters were frightened of her and, as a reaction, concentrated on studying and were always busy reading. They both attached themselves to their father, who introduced them to philosophy and took them with him to the grape harvest and to the cellars to see the new wine being bottled, taught them to drive a car and write good Italian. The servants, fully understanding the situation, laughed at her. All in all, no one liked her, and she responded to this lack of affection by increasing the stridency of her voice.

Towards the end, after her husband had died and her daughters had become alienated from her, she lived alone in Bagheria, eating up the remaining assets of the estate in the sole company of a Pomeranian dog which she loved passionately. To defend herself she kept a gun at her bedside.

She was quite capable of taking the law into her own hands for she was afraid of nothing and no one. If she heard noises in the garden she would lean over the first-floor balcony, her gun under her arm, all ready to shoot. She certainly did not lack courage. She did not ask for any companionship; she proclaimed that she was self-sufficient. On the death of her husband she took her daughters to court to obtain all their inheritance in addition to the share she was entitled to. An indomitable enemy of the rest of the family, she was reduced to a solitary existence in one wing of the villa, having as friends various odd characters from the village: an old school teacher, a retired farmer with whom she would play cards late into the night. Together they would drink iced anise while gossiping about the evils of the world. Every day a gardener would pick great bunches of flowers to cheer up the solitary room, a bedroom, in which she was reduced to living.

One night, she was within a hair's breadth of shooting at my father with the gun she always kept loaded. It was at the time when we were still living in the former stables. My father, unable to sleep, had gone into the garden for a walk. My grandmother heard him and came out on to the balcony carrying her gun. Luckily my father saw her and shouted 'Sonia, it's me!' And she, after having yelled heaven knows what insults, went back to bed. But the next day she accused my father of having gone out to steal eggs from her hens.

My mother detested her for this petty spitefulness, and she would go for months without addressing a word to her. It was not until a few years ago, when my grandmother went into hospital after having broken her hip, that my mother was able to put her ill feelings on one side and look after her like a loving daughter.

Recently my mother told me how 'at the end of her life she gave out a terrible smell from her bedsores. But she was completely unaware of this. She used to sleep with the key of the safe attached to her wrist by a small piece of string. She didn't trust anyone, not even me. I wanted to say to her "Mama, I'm not interested in your money, I'm here to make my peace with you before you die." But she watched me with those dark eyes of hers, shining with fever, and she didn't understand. . . . She never understood anything, she was a barbaric savage only able to have trust in herself, like a wild animal of the forest. Her problem was having to live the life of an aristocrat when she was born to exhibit herself on the stage. But this was forbidden her, and out of this denial came her mediocre little household theatricals for which we, her daughters, never forgave her. But I didn't want her to die like a dog. When I saw her eventually giving up, her face ravaged by illness, her eyes fading away, I felt so much pity for her; I wanted to take her in my arms like a child, for that was what she had been all her life, to console her, to sing softly one of those Chilean songs she loved so much.'

She died leaving only a few crumbs of what had once been a large fortune. To me she left a small piece of nineteenth-century furniture with little Egyptian heads carved in light red wood, and a dress of fuchsia-red silk with big embroidered pockets which I have kept as a relic of the theatre.

AUNT Saretta taps her foot to arouse me from my day-dreams. Her long amber necklace dances on her chest. The dark patches on her neck and arms seem to come alight with an intense, threatening brown colour.

We go out on to the terrace. The old blue and white tiles are still there, the same as when I left them so many years ago. A sharp pain grips my throat, the memory of a warm summer night comes back to me when, stretched out on those tiles, my father, a friend of his from Tuscany and I gazed with fascination at the sky sprinkled with stars. All around us the air was soft and scented. Above us so many glittering jewels. 'Just think,' said my father, 'below us is the earth, and below that the void . . . and here we are suspended, rushing towards something we can never know.'

He turned towards his friend rather than towards me. I was still too much of a child to be involved in the mysteries of the universe. Every so often a small wave of disquieting scent wafted towards us; the jasmine was barely in flower.

Years later I planted jasmine on my terrace in Rome. In summer I watch for the flowers to open, waiting to gather in their scent. But each time is a disappointment. The perfume is there but it is so faint and lightly scented that it has nothing of the almost painful intensity of the jasmine in Bagheria; nourished by another kind of soil, moist and harsh, bathed by water that is scarcer but perhaps more concentrated, caressed by hot winds from Africa, it develops an exquisitely sensuous perfume. If I were able to stay alive for a few days while waiting for death, I would choose the jasmine of Bagheria, just as Democritus chose fresh bread. (His sister was getting married and he did not want to spoil the festivities, so he kept himself alive by sniffing fresh bread.)

Yet it certainly did not take much to spoil the scent from that jasmine at the Villa Valguarnera: the faint odour of chicken manure that came from the henhouse at the bottom of the garden, or the rank stench of flayed skins which the shepherds hung to dry right in front of the gates of the villa, would transform the scent into something overpowering that tainted the whole atmosphere.

But that night when my father's friend had arrived from Florence to stay, the air was clean and the perfume coming from these small flowers the colour of milk was now mingled only with the smell of the sleeping mint that sprouted up between the tiles, and the faint breath of salt water wafting up from the wide expanse of sea beyond Monte Zafferano.

I listened in silence to the exchanges of words and ideas between my father and his childhood friend, relieved they were not excluding me from the discussion. To some extent

I felt part of their speculative world, of their questioning of language and their searching imaginations.

'And suppose the universe breathed?'

I don't recollect whether it was my father or his young friend who spoke. Putting their ages together would only add up to fifty-five. Needless to say, I had fallen in love with that friend and was gawking at him and listening longingly with my ears and my eyes wide open. I was fascinated by him because he was so utterly different from me: lean, dark, with something arabic about his luminous black eyes.

'Suppose we were part of the long pause between the act of breathing in and the act of breathing out?'

I envied his intimacy with my father, something of the solidarity that only men are able to initiate amongst themselves because of their ancient sense of comradeship, and so create a distillation of free ideas.

'If there is breath there must also be a thinking being, a God.'

'You're trying to make sense out of something that has none. There is no thought behind that breath, only a manifestation of life. It's just fortuitous.' My father pressed on in his beautiful calm voice, the 'c's' a little aspirated.

'How can you be so sure?'

'I don't know, I imagine it. But imagination, nourished by experiences, is conserved over time. . . . I know it because Heraclitus said it to Taletus and Taletus said it to Galileo and Galileo said it to Newton and Newton said it to Locke and Locke to Hume and Hume to Hegel and Hegel said it to Marx, who whispered it in a low voice into my ear.'

'Marx can never have said that because Marx declared philosophy was dead.'

'Perhaps he didn't say it, but he suggested it to Einstein and Einstein wrote how time does not exist. . . .'

'And where are you going to put all those awkward people like Plato, Campanella, Pascal, Heidegger, Nietszche, who all dream of gods and men philandering happily together?'

And here I heard a small, almost imperceptible laugh followed by a sniff that made me aware of the superiority of reason over the pretensions of faith, that dry radical reasoning I knew inhabited the mind of the man whom I had loved and lost and who was my father.

But Aunt Saretta is still tapping her foot, impatient to get back to her game of cards and obviously full of suspicion towards this niece who has spat on the family, spat on the nobility, spat on faith, proclaimed heretical ideas, and has been connected with dangerous Socialist groups, impertinently treading underfoot the ancient principles of hierarchy.

I see her taking note of my canvas shoes, my worn cotton jeans, my striped shirt and my bag with its shoulder strap. She gives me a pitying smile; to her it is clear that only clumsy, disorderly and specious thoughts can exist in the head of anyone dressed like me.

But hiding her prejudices, she takes us into the abandoned gardens. The goddess Ceres, carrying a cornucopia, is lying on the ground decapitated; the coffee house of enamelled ironwork tilts to one side, with ants running busily along its rusted iron grilles, the floor is split and upturned by the invasive roots of a false acacia that has encroached on the garden, its suckers forcing themselves spontaneously out of the general dereliction.

In that coffee house, Don Pietro Ucrìa di Scannatura, the husband of Marianna Ucrìa, was in the habit of retiring to sip his morning coffee and contemplate with opaque gaze his estate, which spread down towards the sea. And Marianna watched him from the first-floor window where, two hundred years later, lived my Grandmother Sonia, who came from Chile and was married to one of the last Dukes of Salaparuta.

I notice how the parapet wall of tufa stone that encloses the garden has been hacked to pieces and has partly collapsed. Bits of the balustrade have fallen down in the direction of the valley. On one side, where one used to be able to see the slope of a gentle hill of wheat, all rough and grey like the skin of an elephant, there is a gap in the stones in the centre of which stands an ugly, newly built mansion the colour of sugared almonds. The hill has been disembowelled, the trees uprooted and destroyed, the countryside pointlessly desecrated.

Turning my gaze towards the sea, I note with relief that the olive trees are still there, a mass of them, still with the same silvery colour. Between the olives, down to the right, is the Villa Spedalotto, with its slender columns, its sunny courtyard that is always empty, and its gate always shut.

The Marquis of Paterno di Spedalotto acquired the villa from the Lord of Arezzo while it was still being built. The small country house consisted of a farm building restored and transformed towards the end of the century to serve as a summer residence. One came to it through a portico which is reached by a gate opening on to the old country road which crosses the Via Consulare at Solunto. The building rises in the midst of a slope of perfumed olive groves which reach almost as far as the hills of Montagnola di Serra di Falco, in the Despuches district close to the watering trough of the same name. The house is built in a style between Louis XII and Neoclassicism: it has an additional storey and a chapel with a sacristy.

Thus writes the most seraphic Girgenti in his didactic prose, touched by the loving appreciation he demonstrates towards the smallest architectural building in his native Bagheria.

The Bourbon Ferdinando XI, the nefarious King Bomba, also noted for his cruelty and treachery, was born in Bagheria, in the Villa Arezzo. His father, Francesco I, a villain even more fierce and brutal than his son, often stayed at the villa with his Queen. An epigraph, still there, records their hospitality in Arezzo during the months of October, November, and December in the year 1799.

'It is said', continues our well-meaning Girgenti,

that in the small Villa Arezzo Spedalotto, the cradle in which the infant who would become the barbarous King Bomba let out his first whimperings is still kept. . . . In 1850, Victor Hugo, haranguing the crowd on the eve of the historic expedition of the thousand in Sicily, said, 'Cape Mongerbino ends in a deserted beach. On that beach gendarmes are carrying sacks in which they have tied men up. They plunge the sacks into the water and hold them down until there is no more struggling, then they pull the sack out and say to the man inside: "Confess". If he refuses, they throw the sack back into the water. It was in this way that Giovanni Vienna da Messina was murdered.'

My maternal forebears, who today look down with indifferent eyes from the pictures hanging on the walls, would certainly have grabbed hold of the sack, and if they were not on the beach to push it down into the water with their own hands, they would without any doubt have been at home eating sweetmeats and sorbets while someone else was tightening up the sacks with strong tough string on their behalf.

This did not prevent their lord- and ladyships from indulging in precious sentiments and elevated thoughts. Many, like Giovanni Alliata, harpsichord player and composer, 'third Prince di Villafranca, Duke of Sala di Paruta, professor of literature and patron of virtuosi, wrote agreeable poems in the Italian and Sicilian languages, so that he was accepted by the literary *Repubblica*, and Canon Antonio Maggiore makes honourable mention of him in his bibliography'.

*84*

But the majority of the family were justices of the peace, jurists, magistrates, senators, deputies, bishops. In 1757, one member of the family was made director of the postal services in Sicily, representative of the Viceroy and Procurator-at-arms.

The postal service brought many advantages to the Alliata family, who reinvested in trust funds, vineyards, and large mansions right up to the end of the nineteenth century. After that, decadence set in and it is certain that by the end of the Second World War they were up to their necks in debt.

A MONG the many noblemen who attended the
marriage, Francesco Alliata stood out, not only on
account of the gallant appearance of his own person as
well as that of his horses and livery, but also because of
his bravura and skill; he earned the most applause and
the most acclaim in all the games that were played before
the Princess of the Royal House. . . . His innate nobility
of character was apparent when he restored the Grotto of
Santa Rosalia on Monte Pellegrino at Palermo in the year
of Our Lord 1603.

Earlier still, there was Filippaccio Alliata who died in 1364 leaving his wife Ursula and five children. Their son Gerardo established himself in Palermo and had a sister, Sigismonda, who became a nun in the convent of San Geronimo of the Order of San Domenico. . . . Then Sigismonda decided to donate her dowry and chattels to the said convent so as to enlarge and embellish it as happened with the miraculous image of the Most Holy Virgin of Pity, which had been kept by the nuns inside a coffer in a hidden place. A plaintive voice was heard to issue from that very same chest and the said image was restored to the church with pomp and ceremony. No more was heard and so it was called the church and convent of the Madonna of Pity. Many noble damsels took part, wishing to become nuns, and because the space in the convent was very confined Frederico Abatelli on his death bequeathed them his own palace, of which vestiges still remain at Parlatorio, and where Sigismonda lived for many years as a true and observant nun. She became Abbess of the convent and died with the reputation of sanctity and perfection.

All this hit me in the face when I read the book by Aunt Felicita, who had herself rewritten another book of the seventeenth century with a view to making it better known and preserving the history of the Alliata di Salaparuta family. A mass of flattery and bragging: according to the author, a family of noble and courageous individuals, always ready to donate money to build new chapels, to set off and kill the 'Moorish traitors', or to take sides with the Spanish Royalty, full of pretensions and arrogance, the haughty nobles with magnanimous hearts and fastidious feelings.

I thought I had thrown them all out of my life by an act of will: I had never visited my Sicilian relatives except for Aunt Felicita, when I was a child, and gentle Uncle Quinto, a great preserver of family history and a sensitive pianist.

I never thought about the past, I was never interested in knowing where those villas and estates had come from: luckily they no longer belonged to us but only remained as a memory of lost magnificence. I thought of them as alien, with all the prejudices of my young bourgeois heart. I belonged to my father and to my English grandmother who had abandoned her husband and three daughters and left her home to roam as far as Baghdad, and then got married for love in Florence to my grandfather, the sculptor Antonio Maraini.

I knew all too well the arrogance and cruelty of the mafia, which the important aristocratic families of Sicily had nourished and caused to prosper because they made laws for their own benefit against the peasants, without the least concern about the methods the farmers were using in their name: closing their eyes to the abuses, torture, and the limitless arrogance that went on right under their noses but discreetly out of range of their sensitive ears.

I did not want to have anything to do with them. To me they were unknown strangers. I had already disowned them forever when I was nine years old, and had come back from Japan starving and destitute, my idiot cousin death shrouded at the back of my eyes.

Neither did I want to hear them talked about. I considered the Villa Valguarnera, where I had indeed lived for a number of years, to be already lost – and good riddance: I would not have wanted it even if it had been given to me. With an icy and dismissive gesture I pushed aside the memories of my heart as if they were simply burdens, remnants of the ingenuous world of childhood.

I was on the side of my father, who had given a kick in the teeth to the stupidities of those arrogant princes by turning down the title of Count, his due as the husband of the eldest daughter of the Duke who left no other heirs.

My father had taken my mother's hand and carried her off to Fiesole to starve, far from the quarrels of her anxious and unbending family. When they got married they sent round an announcement of their wedding which consisted of a small drawing of themselves in the nude seen from behind on a deserted beach. And this created scandal and indignation among the relations.

As for me, I saw myself as having been born out of my father's head like a new Minerva, armed with pen and paper and ready to confront the world through the difficult task of working with the alchemy of words.

And my mother? She had given a kick to that past too. But she never spoke of it. She gave a wide berth to her countless relations; above all to those of the preceding generation, for the cousins seemed to be as uncertain and intolerant as her. Cousin Quinto, Cousin Manina, and Cousin Fiammetta were delicate and defenceless, and similarly in flight from an ancestry too burdensome. The others, the elderly, seemed closed like oysters, long since dead and dried up inside the precious shells in which they believed they could keep their pearls forever simply by closing their serrated valves.

What remains of all that magnificence? Palaces falling to bits, rusty mirrors, chipped chandeliers with crusts of old wax candles that can no longer be removed.

And the children of the children's children? People who struggled between old debts and new debts, overwhelmed by suicidal depression or mad delusions of grandeur – enough to make one wash one's hands of them forever.

And yet, there they are, they have landed on my shoulders all together, with a clatter of old bones, at the moment when I made the decision to write about Sicily after years of putting it off and rejecting it. Not of an imaginary or a literary Sicily, stuff of my dreams, magnified into myth; but of the spoiling of brocade dresses, of those stagnant portraits, of those rooms reeking of a sour staleness, of those faded wallpapers, those vanishing scandals, those old, old stories that are only a part of me, but still do belong to me and cannot be driven away

*89*

like aggravating flies just because I have decided that they irritate me.

I had written eight novels before writing *The Silent Duchess*, always avoiding like the plague the island of jasmine flowers and tainted fish, of sublime hearts and razor-sharp knives. Only in a few poems published by Feltrinelli in 1968 (and now out of print) did I speak of Palermo or of Bagheria. But it was an intense, bitter dialogue between me and myself, filtered through the ever-present spectre of a father both loved and repudiated.

To talk of Sicily means opening a door that has remained bolted, a door I have camouflaged so well with climbing plants and a tangle of leaves as to forget that it had ever been there: a wall, a closed and impenetrable barrier.

Then a hand, a hand I do not recognize, growing out of an unbuttoned and forgotten sleeve – a very bold hand, full of curiosity – began to push against that door, pulling down the spiders' webs and pulling up the twining roots. Once it was open, I peered into a world of memories, feeling slightly sick and full of suspicion. . . . The ghosts I saw pass by certainly did not entice me. But I was there and I could not draw back.

This return has been stimulated by a renewed contact with some friends from Palermo with whom I had lost touch: Marilù, with her ironic pungent wit, the gentle, thoughtful Bice, the generous-hearted Giuseppe with his manic intelligence. And all those behind them – Francesco, Roberto, Nino, Marie Pie, Gabriella, Giglio – whom I had lost sight of for so many years.

I don't know whether it was they who brought me to this door, or whether it was the open door itself that enabled me to catch sight of them there, still alive, among the ghosts of people who have disappeared. It could also be age playing its usual tricks, bringing close what is at a distance and pushing away what is close. I have been driven by an overpowering compulsion to reread long-forgotten authors: Verga, Capuana, Meli, Pitrè, Villabianca, Mortillaro and lastly, the most loved of all, De Roberto.

So it is that I have started to go back to Palermo, in spite of the horror I feel for the havoc of new building: a physical horror, a total and decisive refusal of my body to adjust to the unbelievable vulgarity of the new developments.

Each time it is the same. I go down to Aspra, I see the arrogant little villas that stretch out along the rocks where once chair-menders used to sit, using their toes to twist the beaten fibres of the agave plant, and my soul turns over in revolt. I go to Bagheria, and I see how they have destroyed half the countryside to bring the new motorway blazing right up to the houses, knocking down old gardens, demolishing pillars and capitals and age-old trees, and my throat tightens.

I go up to the Villa Palagonia and I see they have run up buildings any old how, one after another, with horrifying haste, right behind those lovely statues of tufa stone, marvels of the wonderful imagination of the Sicilian Baroque, and my insides turn over. My whole body is in turmoil but what can I do about it?

I cast a glance at the smart pointed shoes Aunt Saretta is wearing. She has small, well-shaped feet: no bunions like my Grandmother Sonia, whose shoes developed a bulge right down one side towards the end of her life. And my mother has bunions on her feet too, though they are much less noticeable; it is one of the few things in which I have not taken after her. Perhaps I inherited my feet from my other grandmother Yoi, the pilgrim from England. And with her feet I have inherited her passion for wandering.

Aunt Saretta goes in front of me towards the centre of the terrace where it opens on to the garden pool, with Neptune sitting disconsolately in the middle. The fountain has been dry ever since I have known it. During the summer little red and yellow dates fall into it from the palm tree standing right alongside.

Inedible fruit, these dates, too small and bitter to melt in the mouth as the plump sweet ones that come from Libya and Morocco do. Yet the tree must have been introduced from such places, who knows how long ago, to brighten up the courtyards and squares of Sicilian towns. Once we ate so many of them, Pasolini and I, that we both got stomach-ache, and Alberto watched us, sitting on a folding chair in the middle of a beach, laughing at us and at our greediness. But that is another story – I am digressing as if I were drunk.

I cast another glance at Aunt Saretta's sharply pointed shoes so as not to look at the palm tree, because I have suddenly caught a glimpse of appalling new buildings: a shoddy block of ten storeys thrown up with a minimum of decent taste, and who knows how many fatalities.

Bagheria is a mafioso town. Everybody knows this but it must never be alluded to. In the sixties I was taken to court on the grounds that I had made one of my characters say that Bagheria was mafioso. But the proceedings got abandoned along the way and it was never brought to a conclusion; probably because it would have been too difficult to prove I was lying at a time when all the newspapers were full of people being murdered without anyone knowing how or by whom. Particularly as the small local paper was crammed full of violence, rapes, intimidations, woundings and killings.

This does not mean that there are not many modest, upright and courageous people in Bagheria. I know a group of resolute women who gather together round Antonella Nasca, the lively owner of a chemist's shop. And I think, too, of the many celebrated sons of Bagheria, such as the artist Guttoso, or Buttita or Giuseppe Tornatore. And the indomitable Antonio Morreale, who quietly teaches in a secondary school in Bagheria and at the same time has never ceased to cast an acute and intelligent glance at the past and present of this volcanic town. I have also known many decent-hearted young people who have set up pressure groups, alternative newspapers and associations of vigilantes in Bagheria. The future of the town lies in their hands.

Now we approach the wing where Aunt Felicita used to live. The magnificent rubber plant is losing its leaves which are as fat and juicy as pieces of flesh. Its roots have split open the floor of the terrace and push out hard and knotted among the abandoned drain pipes. Here there is also a fountain, with traces of water lilies and slimy water now choked with leaves; where goldfish used to swim there are now only pieces of guttering that have fallen off the roof.

From the north, the houses of the new violated Bagheria come lapping the walls of the garden of the Villa Valguarnera. In a few years, if it continues, the gardens will be swallowed up along with the rest of the ground and will end by reducing the villa to a stump lost in a desert of concrete, and the town will have destroyed for ever one of its most precious architectural memories.

The municipality of Bagheria is rich but the conservation of its artistic wealth has remained until now the least of its concerns. I can't predict whether the villa will be bought by some public body or by a private company, after what I saw in Palermo, when a public institution bought a theatre with an undertaking that they would put it to rights: they ripped off the roof and then, only a few months later, suspended all work on it so that the building was left to go to rack and ruin. It was abandoned to the wind and rain and became derelict within a year.

Moreover, the family themselves have yielded to the pressure of debts, and abandoned a large part of the garden and sold it. What will be the fate of our magical, dreamlike baroque roots? Will our protestations amount to no more than flinging ourselves at a windmill with a tin sword?

From this little wall of tufa stone, now threatened by the large housing development of a crowded Bagherian suburbia, I once witnessed a firework display that 'married' the hand of man to that of nature. . . . One night, maybe in 1948 or '49, in the corner of a room, a woman with a freckled face lay ill, her eyes lost in a scared sadness yet restored to life by a crazy joy. She was expecting her fifteenth child and staying in bed as the doctors had ordered. Her previous fourteen children had all died before birth, and each time they had carried away a piece of her body. Every so often it would return to life, and with hopeful yearning she would offer hospitality to another small infant, and then for some unaccountable reason would suddenly expel it as if she hated it.

The husband, in thick pebble glasses, his hair like a tower on his head, walked up and down crumbling a cigarette between his broad, swollen fingertips. . . .

That night we were outside, leaning against the balustrade in a part of the garden that did not belong to us to watch the famous fireworks of Bagheria, which brought people from as far away as Cefalù or Misilmeri. It was summer, the sun had not long gone down and there were still streaks of pink floating along the horizon, violet smudges that minute by minute were swallowed up by the deepening night.

All at once a field of lilies came into flower in front of us, scintillating petals that shone for a moment in all their brilliance and then went out with a whistle and fell headlong towards the earth. Afterwards, a sudden boom, followed by the apparition of an emerald-green dome, which for a moment was transformed into the silvery vault of a church and then immediately into a handful of rubies that exploded high up in the sky and fell back to earth trailing a little rivulet of white smoke.

They were fireworks in honour of San Giuseppe, patron saint of Bagheria. To pay for the festival, the people of Bagheria, between bewailing their extreme poverty, would bleed themselves regularly year after year. Three families of firework producers were paid lavishly to throw themselves into a brilliant contest, of which the public would act as the sole judge.

In the meantime, the main street was lit up by a thousand coloured lights. Hundreds of stalls, encircled by decorative garlands of red and silver paper, were scattered gaily along the streets, selling snacks of all sorts, pumpkin and sunflower seeds, hazel-nuts, chick-peas, salted almonds, caramellized nuts as well as ice-creams from the country, melon water ices, *sfinciuni, cucuzzate, cannoli*, and liquorice in plaits, bows and little sticks.

Then, all of a sudden, without a breath of wind, there was a rumble of thunder, and the sky was ripped open by long arrows shaped like golden twigs and branches.

Something never seen before, never even dreamed of, a game of lightning that mingled with the firework display and outshone it. A product of human invention in competition with the capricious inventions of nature, a duel which we watched transfixed with wonder.

Fireworks in Sicily end with what has come to be called the *mascoliata finale* – as if to express an outpouring of exuberant male virility, an imitation of coitus which expresses a masculine defiance towards heaven and towards the world.

Then bang, bang, bang, and the fireworks whirled, sprinkling sparks and mingling green flowers and red stars while a shower of snowflakes shrouded in a quivering gauze veiled the dark depths of the night.

Just at that moment, as if it had been summoned by the thunder of the fireworks, the real thunder began, shaking the earth and taking aim at the sky, and the rifts became longer, slashing the sky. It was terrifying to stand beneath the trees that seemed likely to be uprooted at any moment. But we could not tear ourselves away from this extraordinary spectacle, so we stayed to watch the battle played out pitilessly between the fires of earth and the fires of heaven which, after a display of thunder and lightning that lasted for several minutes on end, finally triumphed when the heavens unleashed a stinging deluge of rain. Raindrops as big as chick-peas fell on to the roofs, whipping up the streets and flooding the courtyards in a turmoil of leaves snatched from the ground and strewn in spinning whirls all over the town.

AUNT Saretta's foot is again tapping with impatience and boredom. How is it possible that this girl keeps drifting away from me into her memories? What is the matter with this stupid niece, she seems to be asking herself, that she is so taken over by irrelevant thoughts that she doesn't listen to anything?

'This is a picture by Aunt Felicita,' she tells us. We are in front of a dark painting of large white arum lilies. Although it is painted tentatively, without any real skill, it is brought to life by an innate intelligence. The style is conventional but these lilies suggest there is something more than meets the eye. Awkward and inelegant, they seem to take shape gradually while they are being observed, fantasies of a sensuous dream that fade away into oblivion.

I seem to remember that when Aunt Felicita was young, women were not admitted to art schools. Only occasionally might someone who really persisted a great deal be accepted. But she would not be allowed to join life classes. If she wanted to paint from life she had to choose between dogs, cats and stuffed birds. The female nude was prohibited to women.

Aunt Saretta moves on. But I want to have a better look at this painting. And Bice, whose mother is a good painter, understands and comments on the sensual freshness of these arum lilies.

'Here we have come to the end,' says Aunt Saretta. 'If you want to go and look at the outbuildings' – as she pronounces the word 'outbuildings' she purses her lips a little – 'you can go. I'll wait for you upstairs and we'll have some ices.'

So Bice and I go down to the old stables to take a look at the awful rooms where I lived for three years, and where she too came as a guest just as I used to go to Palermo to stay on the top floor of her father's clinic where I played with her puppets.

I cannot imagine how all five of us managed to live in this small space. The bedroom where my father and mother slept was minute, with a low ceiling. The room where we three sisters used to sleep had a tiny square window looking out on to the hen house, and was hardly any bigger. The living-room was also suitable only for dwarfs, but from it one opened a magic door into the garden. There, in contrast, everything was wide open, spacious, and the views of the horizon receded into the distance.

It was in that house of dwarf rooms that my father was alone one day with the washerwoman, who was nearly eighty years old. The following day the woman's husband came up saying very grumpily that his wife could no longer come to us because we had left her alone with *l'ommu*, the man, and what would people think?

Any woman, beautiful or ugly, old or young, would compromise herself if she remained alone with a man. She would lose her reputation. It was presumed as a matter of course that the man, whether handsome or ugly, young or old, would try to seduce her according to the ancient rules of sexual conquest. What the woman might want would count for absolutely nothing. The woman's choice when faced by a man's desire was not seen to exist. A woman who allowed herself to be left in the company of a man was treated by the family as if she had been raped.

I remember once a woman, a guest of Aunt Orietta, who went for a walk in the country by herself. She met a peasant. He very respectfully offered her a fig. She said 'Yes', and he immediately jumped on top of her. The sole fact of her having replied to his offer was treated as a sign of assent. Since the taking of a woman's body is seen as inevitable and obligatory, the man cannot be held responsible for his abusive behaviour. Rather, it falls to his lot, intentionally or not, the moment he hoists up the flag in his trousers. Such was the philosophy of the men of Bagheria.

A body furnished with a uterus is obliged to hide and deny itself. Any acceptance, even if only a word, a nod, or a moment alone, is seen as an unconditional surrender. Every woman deserted by her man is ruined. Even marriage implies a serious capitulation to the principles of the paternal hierarchy, a surrender from which the woman is unable to escape but which reaffirms her in her fated submission. The surrender cannot take place at once but will be part of an ostentatious ceremonial that will sanction by a public affirmation the possession of the woman's body.

The daughter cannot refuse this act of possession for which the father is always held responsible in every way. Not even when a lascivious father substitutes himself for the husband. Abuse may be criticized, but no one dares to intervene in the relationship of authority between father and daughter, which is very ancient and of all other customs the last to die, even today.

In Bagheria itself there were two obvious cases which everybody knew about, but which would never have been denounced to the authorities. One father had a child by his own daughter. It was public knowledge but at the same time kept a secret. No one knowing about it would have openly admitted it. The wife, married to the father and mother of the girl, behaved as if nothing had happened. The girl went on living with her parents bringing up the baby who was the image of his father.

Another father, living in one of the windowless hovels in the old part of the town, used to abuse his daughter when she was only six, always beneath the averted eyes of the mother. And he went on abusing her as if he had a sacred right, year after year. Then, when the daughter got married at the age of sixteen, he began to abuse the second daughter who was ten. She in her turn grew up but was never able to find anyone to marry her because the first daughter had let something out to her husband and the locals got to hear of it. Then the man turned to the third daughter, making her pregnant and forcing her to have an abortion.

All this happened in the silence of the rooms in a dark little hovel full of precious plates that were used only on feast-days, in one of those enormous high beds beneath which hens often scratched around, in those smoke-filled kitchens where it took half an hour to light the stove in the morning with the energetic use of bellows.

The Church and public morality of course prohibit such physical coupling between father and daughter. But something far more ancient and hidden, which has nothing to do with desire but derives from the expression of primitive power, pushes these men to act in secret according to principles that they hold in their hearts to be right. Is not a daughter flesh of one's own flesh, blood of one's own blood?

The laws of the universe are more ancient and more perfect than the decrees of established morality that have been the accepted way of thinking. But by whom have these laws been established? The claims of the flesh, according to them, come before any laws, human or divine. Did not Lot also act in this way in those famous Bible stories? He lay with his daughters and got them pregnant with children in his own semblance and image. And as for Lot's daughters, what were their names? Every night the insane arrogance of the peasant world rips to pieces everything the rules of bourgeois morality and Catholic morality re-establish by day.

'DID you know that Queen Carolina occupied this room for a week when she stayed here with all her court?'

'I think I've read about it in Aunt Felicita's book.'

'These white and gold consoles with long opaque mirrors were put here for her. At that time the villa didn't have shutters, and do you know what the Queen did? She brought shutters with her because she couldn't stand the light early in the morning. Then when she left she had the shutters taken off their hinges, and carried them away with her. She also removed the stucco coat-of-arms on the inside façade, with its crouching lions and two flags, which you saw as you came in.'

'Why did she do that?' I know the answer but I want to hear it again from her.

Aunt Saretta smiles a sad bitter smile. 'Because of royal pride. She didn't want anywhere she had lived to display a coat-of-arms that wasn't hers. In recompense she left a present to the villa that stayed for years inside a casket, until the burglars made off with it.'

'What was that?'

'A box made of leather from Bulgaria, embossed in gold and lined with blue velvet, with a coffee set for two people: two little cups, a coffee pot and a sugar bowl. On the cups is written *l'espérance soutient le malheureux jusqu'au tombeau.*

But to know more I had to go and consult Aunt Felicita's book.

'On the tray that goes with the little rounded cups which are painted so delicately, *le malheureux* is depicted naked with a small piece of drapery to cover his "shame". One foot is in the grave, while he lifts his trusting gaze towards *l'espérance* who, dressed in a white tunic, supports him on one arm while she holds a lighted lamp with the other hand. It was made and signed by either Capodimonte or Buen Retiro. The subject is not one of the happiest to accompany the sipping of a cup of coffee,' comments my Aunt Felicita slyly.

'Perhaps you know it was here that the marriage was held between Louis Philippe of Orléans, guest at the Villa Spedalotto, and Maria Amelia, daughter of Maria Carolina and Ferdinando Bourbon?'

'Tell me about it, Aunt Saretta. It interests me.'

'From the Villa Spedalotto there was a path leading up to our villa, and every day Louis Philippe, who later became King of France, came along it to visit his sister-in-law the Queen. A sentry always stood by the gate, which gave access from the property to the small flower-beds and hanging gardens high up on the rocks.'

I continue in Aunt Felicita's words, which I find more congenial than Aunt Saretta's:

One evening at dusk as the Duke went by, the sentinel presented arms and let the gun slip out of his hands, and the shot went off in the direction of Louis Philippe who fortunately escaped injury. It was said to have been an accident but it was whispered that this 'accident' happened by order of the Queen. . . . This was not the first time that crimes and poisonings had been attributed to her.

'In truth,' continues Aunt Felicita sagely,

as a woman and as a Queen, Maria Carolina's life was tormented by her frenzied emotions, by the tragic death of her sister Marie-Antoinette, and above all by having a vulgar and selfish husband. All this brought on her paroxysms of rage. In the family, the account of a dinner in honour of Lord and Lady Bentinck still reverberates. They had liberated Grandfather Giuseppe from the island of Pantellaria where he had been in exile on suspicion of sympathy towards Garibaldi and his followers.

Grandfather Giuseppe always had French cooks, but alas the flavour of their dishes no longer reaches me!

It is still Aunt Felicita writing.

The table must have been vast since it was decorated in the centre with a small temple in the Doric mode which is still in existence. It is finely carved in wood with pillars, balustrades, stairs, tripods and statues that are replicated in other smaller temples at the end of the long table. It was all painted in an opaque bluish white. Such monuments seem to have been filled with many small porcelain figures of damsels and shepherds, no longer in the style of Watteau but more like that of Reynolds, due to the English influence which was dominant during that period in Sicily.

The tablecloth, which I have actually seen, is of the finest damask and is all in one piece, about eight metres long. At the end of the room were two plaster figures brilliantly executed by Villareale. The dinner service of finest china could serve sixty guests, and I believe about that number were there. It was of French manufacture from the factory of the Count d'Artois, which was very short-lived although it was thought to rival that of Sèvres. The dinner service comprised around a hundred pieces and was lavish in additional accessories: there were goblets, vases for cooling wine, fruit baskets, pepper pots and salt cellars of various designs ornamented with minute blue fleurs-de-lis and rose-coloured tulips, bordered with laurel leaves and small red berries festooned with loops and scrolls of gilded foliage.

The Prince of Villafranca used to send his linen to Paris to be ironed: cravats, hose, lace and frills. And when he was on his travels he would take with him a special kind of sheet, which I have seen.

Aunt Felicita goes out of her way to describe this with care: 'In cream-coloured chamois leather bordered with ribbons of light blue silk, they could be washed, and took the place of linen sheets.'

There is a photograph of Aunt Felicita seated in a big open car wearing a cloche hat. It must have been taken about 1920. She wears the crafty expression of someone who is in the know and keeps it to themselves: a curious mixture of probing intelligence and childlike innocence. It makes me think of another photograph in a book by Gertrude Stein, *The Autobiography of Alice B. Toklas*, which was of course a fiction because it is Gertrude Stein who is writing. She is talking of herself, looking at herself ironically, delighting in her little dogs, her walking sticks, her pictures, her cooking. Aunt Felicita resembles Gertrude Stein – I've only come to see this recently. They certainly had something in common: they were both well-to-do, and they maintained a free and easy connection with their wealth, keeping an eye on their creature comforts but without overdoing it, not forgetting other people's hardships and privations. Ironic and generous, they exhibited a kind of serene ugliness which can sometimes be seen as deep maternal beauty. Their bodies had become swollen, perhaps through having at some time yielded to a nervous hunger, their feet had grown gigantic, becoming thickset and heavy in order to support their weight when they were walking. Yet there was much grace in the way they moved with a gentle smiling reserve.

And didn't they also share an interest in painting? Gertrude Stein had a more critical spirit and the sense of being a spectator, whereas Aunt Felicita had the attitude of a painter with a more indulgent point of view. Both were lovers of food, animals and woods, and both were in the habit of observing others and themselves, except that Gertrude Stein came from the heart of a society that projected itself optimistically into the future, wedded to its moral principles as well as its transgressions and its controversial declarations against 'immorality', while Aunt Felicita came from the roots of a Mediterranean province with an atavistic sense of insecurity, principles and duty that mixed together the teachings of the Catholic Church with the more licentious hazards of free thought and enlightenment.

Gertrude Stein came from a Jewish family, she was an intellectual full of curiosity and eccentricity. Aunt Felicita came from an aristocratic family who had for centuries believed themselves to be so protected by the gods that they never had to undertake the pain of poking their noses into the affairs of

*107*

the world. They were privileged by the grace of God, and that was that. Amen. It was indeed a miracle that Aunt Felicita was able to be so spontaneous, so searching, and so taken up with the arts. In her book, as in the book on vegetarian cookery written by my Grandfather Enrico, there is the best of Sicily, which has cultivated the bitter art of laughing at itself.

WE are on the first floor, in the large drawing-room that looks out on to the terrace. The walls are not square but have angles, alcoves and niches. But each curve is interrupted by the big French windows which open on to the wide terrace with the blue and white tiles.

Since every object carries the imprint of its time, it is easy to imagine our forebears in large billowing and corseted dresses, wigs high on the heads, faces covered in rice powder, hands intent on telling their rosaries or gripping little cups of chocolate. Even if on closer scrutiny the wigs were often inhabited by lice, the clothes dusty, the bodies weighed down by greasy oily food, the breath made sour by decaying teeth which no one knew how to treat except by pulling them out and leaving the mouth beyond cure.

It is easy to imagine how on these blue and white tiles, barely warm from the first rays of the sun, were set down the slippers of the gentleman of the household, who had just washed his face in a little basin of cold water refined by one single rose petal. Then he would have sat at a small table with legs of cherrywood to drink a cup of coffee, while a valet put on his shoes and another combed his hair and tied it at the back of his neck just as in pictures by Hogarth or Longhi.

And the lady of the household? She too would have just got up, and enveloped herself in a gown of crêpe de Chine to join her husband on the sunlit terrace, and sat down to eat a slice of buttered bread while a servant got ready a tray of toilet preparations for her: face cream by Monsieur Varigault, fresh from Paris, lettuce water scented with orange, burnt cork to outline the eyes, just as my Grandmother Sonia used to do, making her enormous black eyes look as if she were possessed and a little mad.

Aunt Saretta goes over to the balustrade and invites us to look at the view. In the distance the sea opens out like a fan, a pale turquoise blue, light and powdery. On the left, Solunto, the lovely hill where, after the expulsion of the Phoenicians, the Greeks built one of their most civilized cities, whose streets, shops and squares are still recognizable among the ruins today.

Soleus, we are told, was a giant who lived at the summit of Mongerbino. He fed off human flesh and had a preference for young virgins. Sometimes, instead of eating them, he would keep them as concubines and only later, when he got bored with them, would he cut them into pieces and devour them.

The inhabitants of the surrounding hills asked Hercules to come and free them from the gigantic monster. So Hercules, the slayer of great serpents, came to the summit of Mongerbino. He said it was a beautiful place worthy of being inhabited, confronted the giant, throttled him with his short strong arms and threw him into the sea.

The legend says that from that moment the mountain took the name of Solunto from Soleus the giant. Here the Phoenicians built their rich temples in honour of Isis, Baal and Tanith, which were subsequently transformed into temples to Zeus and Poseidon by the Greeks.

The Greeks killed the ancient Carthaginian worshippers of Baal, but in their turn were vanquished and killed by the Romans, who with their fleet took possession of all the major Sicilian ports. The raising of the siege of Solunto after months and months of assault was a moment of murderous frenzy and terror for people who for months had only had a taste of food, an onion divided into four, a little uncooked flour mixed with water because there was no longer any firewood to burn. Was it not just the same for us in the Japanese concentration camp? Nothing to cook and nothing to cook with. In desperation we used to gobble up anything that came within range: a mouse, a small snake, ants. We even tried eating acorns – 'If pigs gobble them up why can't we gobble them up too?' – but they proved absolutely inedible. One day we found a group of pale stunted toadstools underneath some stones. But how could we tell whether they were poisonous or not? So we drew lots as to who would be the guinea pig: he would only eat a small piece, and if after eight hours nothing untoward had happened, then the others would eat them too. The poor 'guinea pig' was throwing up all night and we threw away the toadstools.

Perhaps the citizens of the besieged city of Solunto, barricaded at the top of the mountain, shut into the sacred city while the Greeks pressed them from all sides, had had the same experience with toadstools. Then one night, while they were all sleeping the disturbed sleep of those who are unable to eat and suffer from colic and whistling in the ears, a Greek braver and more impatient than the rest, a little Ulysses with worn sandals and plaited hair, scaled the wall, surprised and killed the two guards, slipped along in the dark to the gate and opened it to let in his own soldiers.

By nine o'clock in the morning Solunto was obliterated by smoke; fires devastated the shops which, in spite of the siege, had continued to sell spoonfuls of lard, a few handfuls of dry grain, some small jugs of wine with wax stoppers.

They set fire to the houses with their poor hearths, they set fire to the public baths, they set fire to the dwellings of the rich with their courtyards full of light and urns full of water; they burned the statues enclosed in wood, they even burned down the famous gymnasium with its mosaic floors depicting hunting scenes, where the elders used to meet to dispute with the young, they burned the pitchers of terracotta that were once full of grain and were now empty, and they burned the stage with its great cedarwood beams.

The Greek soldiers ran through the columns of smoke pursuing those Phoenicians who remained in the city. They seized them, bound them and, grasping a knife, cut their throats with one quick movement of the hand. The women were pinioned against a wall or on to the floor and raped. Then they were sent as slaves to a soldier or to an official as a servant, a concubine, a cook, a drudge, according to the demands of their masters. They had to learn to live with the men who had raped them. Sometimes they bore them children and even ended by feeling affectionate towards the father, forgetting the rancour and their desire for revenge.

I remember a book that describes the complex and ambiguous relationship that can become established between the perpetrator of violence and the person who is his victim. The Argentinian military, after having tortured and killed young women, took on the role of fathers to their children and brought them up as if they were their own, in luxury and with the most generous and possessive love.

*112*

Many of the relations of the *desaparecidos* found this partnership more abhorrent than the tortures undergone by their relatives. They undertook extensive research to find and recover the children of the murdered women abducted by the killers. But paradoxically it turned out that the children, once found, had no wish to return to their real grandparents because they had learned to love their pretended parents and former torturers. What is to be done?

'THE Villa Valguarnera was like a royal palace among the princely houses in the verdant valley,' wrote Pitrè.

The owners kept open house for gentlemen of title and their ladies, friends and dependants, and for their servants and valets to whom they could offer commodious hospitality: the rooms were large, the salons decorated with portraits, pictures and ornaments, the setting artistically arranged with orchards and coppices and hanging gardens and loggias and courtyards and fountains and statues and Montagnola, which is the most delightful of hills and the most charming sanctuary. As one gradually ascends through the changing aspects leading to its summit, the eye gets lost wandering between two promontories jutting out into the turquoise-blue sea set against the far distances of sky-blue light, through small valleys and hillsides sloping down to the coast. Then, as you continue to climb, a Cupid smiles at you invitingly, a Diana welcomes you to the chase, a bacchante is dancing, and a Polyphemus is playing on the pipes as if to make you sing the arietta of Metastasio inscribed at his feet.

Here is the mythology of the Villa Valguarnera as Aunt Felicita experienced it. 'The villa of my dreams,' as she calls it in her book published by Flaccovio in 1949. She would talk intimately to the portraits of her ancestors in a way that was both gracious yet also a little frenzied:

> I spoke to him and it seemed as if he was kindly wanting to reply. . . . I stared at him and he stared back at me smiling! I was looking for marks on the gilding of his finely carved picture frame . . . drops of yellow candle wax that had become hard over the years . . . then I saw the room illuminated by a myriad of wax candles in the sumptuous candelabra of Murano glass . . . on the staircase there were powdered servants and valets in rich livery and downstairs footmen with torches to provide light for the carriages and sedan chairs as they arrived.

Aunt Felicita was really a visionary, like me. Perhaps because of this I can't avoid being influenced by her book. In some way it resembles her arum lilies, the make-believe of a nobility that is all smiles and heroics. Beneath it, unconscious and for that reason difficult to understand, she hides a need to dominate that makes you feel somewhat apprehensive. Aunt Felicita's eyes are neither mean nor arrogant, they are simply the eyes of someone who is adept at inventing reality but is also unexpectedly indulgent towards herself.

Aunt Felicita has been dead for years. Meanwhile Aunt Saretta is here, still alive, and now she claps her hands at a young girl with high heels and varnished nails who brings in a tray of goblet-shaped glasses filled with cold lemon tea. She offers us ices from Bagheria on a precious antique salver; very small flowers of ice-cream coated in the finest chocolate. Holding one of them between my finger and thumb, I place it on my tongue and let it melt in my mouth. The fragrance rises sweet and yearning.

We return to the drawing-room and my eyes fall on the large portrait of an ancestor, which I vaguely remember from my wanderings through the villa as a child. It is she, Marianna, life-size, clothed in a stiff ceremonial dress, with the Maltese Cross worn by the nobility on her breast. Her hair is puffed up and powdered; on it a faded rose stands out conspicuously. There is something resolute and despairing in her large clear eyes. Her shoulders are covered, her arms draped in transparent sleeves.

In her book Aunt Felicita writes admiringly of this portrait.

Most elegant in her crinoline, her slender waist is drawn to a point on her dress of silver brocade with its delicate patterning in the softest colours. From the opening at her neck to below her waist a large silver cross is embroidered on a triangle of black velvet, the distinctive Maltese Cross, which only those of the purest descent with four heraldic quarters are privileged to wear. She has large diamonds in her ears and others scattered randomly on her lightly powdered and puffed-out hair, which leaves her wide forehead uncovered, a rose to one side. A big diamond ring on her finger and no other jewellery. She holds a sheet of paper in her hand, for writing was the only way she could express herself: she was called 'the dumb one'.

116

Aunt Felicita was born in 1876, so as a child, she could have known Marianna's niece. Between her and the nineteenth century was not such a long time. It was less than a hundred years since Marianna's death.

Her name, Felicita, has recurred many times in the history of the family. She was named after a baby girl who had died at the age of three a short while before she was born. One of the last photographs of her shows her seated inside a long black Studebaker with a large cloche hat of dark felt on her head. Green, perhaps – knowing her tastes – or possibly midnight blue. The photograph is in black and white. Aunt Felicita looks comical in this luxurious car, as if she were gazing round to say, 'Excuse my daring, but I really love fast driving!' She looks decidedly ugly, with large prominent features, an autocratic nose, a fleshy mouth and a trace of down on her upper lip.

Towards the end of her life she lived in a dark shabby room cluttered with her paintings, always sunk into a ramshackle armchair, its leather threadbare and scratched by her cats.

From time to time as children we would go to her room and get her to tell us a story and she would bewitch us with her deep, spellbinding voice. When she laughed it became silvery and untamed, like the voice of a young peasant girl ingenuous and happy, imprisoned in her old fat, flabby body. Her hands, which were like my mother's and also mine, euphemistically called 'pianist's hands' because they are strong, small, active and excitable: they gesticulate with rapid decisive movements to match the rhythm of words.

She too was fascinated by the deaf-mute Marianna, the distant ancestor with gentle intense eyes who had learned to write so that she could communicate with her family.

'This one was Marianna's husband, her uncle, Pietro Valguarnera e Gravina Palagonia. In the family they used to call him "the prawn" because he always used to dress in red.' A gloomy face, with obscure shadowy thoughts, his eyes deep-set, his mouth curved, his body thin and misshapen. He

117

does not look like a happy man, or one who could make others happy, but without doubt tormented and tormenting.

In her book Aunt Felicita writes of another Alliata, Giovanna, daughter of Giuseppe Alliata Moncada, who in 1864 married her uncle Girolamo Valguarnera, Prince of Ganci. But subsequently all traces of her have been lost. What kind of a family custom was it that gave young girls in marriage to their uncles?

Giovanna, the child-wife, was the sister of Edoardo, father of Felicita: consequently the aunt of my great-aunt. The elder brothers of Edoardo died, so that Edoardo, while still a boy, became head of the family. And in 1830 he married a certain Felicita Lo Faso di San Gabriele. This was how the name 'Felicita' came into the family.

I turn from the portrait of Pietro Valguarnera e Gravina Palagonia to concentrate my eyes on Marianna. Aunt Saretta goes on talking about other ancestors but I am not listening to her. There is something in that portrait of Marianna which worries me: it is the way she is so stiff in a rigid artificial pose that is in contrast to her restless vivacious eyes. But I know that once again it is a matter of theatre. I am faced by something artificial, caught in the ambiguity and amusement of a century that loved the profound transformations accompanying self-caricature.

Marianna constructed for herself – it is sufficient to look carefully at the portrait – a shell of unapproachable severity. Yet her expression shows a profound and forbearing wisdom that she cannot hide beneath 'good manners'. Her eyes are clear and luminous, barely crossed by any cloud of fear.

One can imagine those hands always moving – above all when they are writing they seem to be intent on searching for the meaning of things. A slight wrinkling of the lips suggests the idea of a restrained smile, laughing at its own severity and inconsolable grief: a mixture of intellectual curiosity and dreamy longings, of disciplined severity and ancient, voluptuous whisperings.

Meanwhile the ices of Bagheria are melting on my plate, shedding transparent droplets.

'Have another,' says Aunt Saretta in a friendly manner. But my throat has closed. I am turned to stone, gazing at that portrait as if I recognized it from the deepest part of myself, as if I have been waiting for years to find myself face to face with this woman who has been dead for two centuries, and who holds between her fingers a small sheet of paper on which is written some part, lost and unknown, of my Sicilian past.